T0288748

# THE AGENDA

THE AGENDA

# THE AGENDA

## What Trump Should Do in His First 100 Days

## Joel B. Pollak

author of *Red November* and coauthor of *How Trump Won*

## FOREWORD BY STEPHEN K. BANNON

Skyhorse Publishing

War Room Books may be purchased in bulk at special discounts for sales promotion, corporate gifts, fund-raising, or educational purposes. Special editions can also be created to specifications. For details, contact the Special Sales Department, Skyhorse Publishing, 307 West 36th Street, 11th Floor, New York, NY 10018 or info@skyhorsepublishing.com.

War Room Books® is a registered trademark of WarRoom, LLC. Skyhorse Publishing® is a registered trademark of Skyhorse Publishing, Inc.®, a Delaware corporation.

Visit our website at www.skyhorsepublishing.com.

Please follow our publisher Tony Lyons on Instagram @tonylyonsisuncertain

10 9 8 7 6 5 4 3 2 1

Library of Congress Cataloging-in-Publication Data is available on file.

Hardcover ISBN: 978-1-64821-116-4
eBook ISBN: 978-1-64821-117-1

Jacket design by David Ter-Avanesyan

Printed in the United States of America

*In memory of Rhoda Kadalie*

# CONTENTS

# Foreword
## by Stephen K. Bannon

Let me first say that Joel Pollak is one of the most talented writers or editors I have ever met. He was Breitbart's first editor-in-chief when the site launched, right up through Andrew Breitbart's untimely death in March 2012. Joel brings his extraordinary talent to this book.

The first 100 days of any US president's administration are critical . . . and most administrations usually don't get it right the first time. Historically, the notion for this metric was invented by Franklin D. Roosevelt, who created new jobs, stabilized farm prices, signed major budget cut legislation, and created the Tennessee Valley Authority—a regional energy project that brought power to neglected rural areas—all in his first 100 days.

Again, the history of this presidential benchmark is not burdened by many successful achievements. An exception is President Ronald Reagan. He signed a major budget cut package, filled with executive branch cuts. Here is one quote about his first 100 days; "Mr.

Reagan has established his goals faster, communicated a great sense of economic urgency and come forward with more comprehensive proposals than any new president since the first 100 days of Franklin D. Roosevelt."

And that celebratory assessment came from—wait for it—*The New York Times*.

Most candidates try to prepare for the transfer of power, with countless opinions from outside "transition experts," historians, journalists, academics, lawyers, etc. But let's face facts. Would you, despite whatever successful background you have or education you possess, know how to staff a White House, run the vast federal government, and lead the United States on day one?

Especially, perhaps, when media pollsters confidently predicted you would lose the election?

And that is why this book is an instant American classic.

Joel was once a Tea Party-backed candidate for Congress in Illinois. Born in South Africa, he was a political speechwriter and holds a master's degree from the University of Cape Town. He also holds a bachelor's degree and a law degree from Harvard University and was a fellow at the Hudson Institute. The list of awards he's won, and the number of important books he's written, is lengthy.

But let's focus on this book, which may be the most important book he has ever written.

Joel has laid out a specific set of purposeful tasks and

priorities that President Trump and his administration must accomplish in the first 100 days. Critically, he notes that many of these tasks can be put into action without cooperation from a Congress that is rarely completely reliable.

In the following chapters, Joel lays out the actions that the president must take in the first 100 days of his next Administration. The recommendations are broad in some instances, with pinpoint specificity in others.

Among the recommendations:

- Revoke the security clearances of every one of the fifty-one former national security and intelligence officials who signed a letter that falsely claimed the Hunter Biden laptop was "Russian disinformation."
- Federalize the National Guard in border states to assist Border Patrol until urgent immigration reforms can be enacted.
- Impose strong sanctions on China and Chinese businesses linked to those that produce fentanyl.

Joel Pollak correctly notes that, in November, "a victorious Trump will have completed the greatest political comeback in American history and will have the opportunity to make the kinds of big changes that come along once in a generation."

Let's get to work to save this country.

# Author's Note

The idea for this book came to me—or returned to me—on the morning of Saturday, June 1, the day after former President Donald Trump was convicted on flimsy charges in a sham trial before a partisan judge and a biased jury in New York City. (As cartoonist Scott Adams observed, the phrase "trumped-up charges" existed long before the trial, but now will forever be linked to the former president, since that is what he has faced—not just in Manhattan, but everywhere.)

Like many Americans—and not just Trump supporters—I felt deeply frustrated. Knowing that Trump would likely benefit politically from the unjust verdict did not mitigate that sense of anger, the feeling that this abuse of the legal system for political ends was profoundly un-American. I did not know what to do about it; I am a lawyer, but I am not Trump's lawyer, and even Trump's attorneys had had little recourse except to file appeals and petitions, and wait for the wheels of the system to turn.

I was home alone with my three children; my wife, pregnant with our fourth child, was away at her college reunion. My eight-year-old son coaxed me outside to play catch—he is an avid baseball player—and it was in the course of tossing the ball back and forth in our yard that an idea occurred to me: I could respond by laying out Trump's governing agenda. What better way to get back at the crooked prosecutors than to presume Trump's victory, and describe it?

I remembered that I had recently suggested a book idea to my agent, Keith Urbahn of Javelin, laying out a possible agenda for Trump's second term. The idea came rushing back to me, and I allowed it to percolate over the course of the day. When I had finally fed the children, put them to bed, and cleaned up the kitchen, I sat down to write. You are holding the result—the product of ten days of intense work, a chapter per day, amidst a busy news cycle.

I do not work for the Trump campaign, nor did I consult the Trump campaign in writing it. I did not even look through Trump's speeches or policy statements or press releases to check that my ideas lined up with his. No one on the campaign reviewed or edited this book. I based my suggestions on what I know about his preferences, and what I have learned about American politics as senior editor-at-large for Breitbart News, where I have worked for over thirteen years.

I have written about Trump before—not just in the

ordinary course of political coverage, but also in previous books. My 2017 book, *How Trump Won: The Inside Story of a Revolution*, co-authored with historian Larry Schweikart, was one of the first books to emerge about the 2016 election. Consequently, it sold very well. One Trump supporter even gave it to the president for him to sign: the Associated Press published a photo of Trump holding it aloft, enjoying the title.

In 2020 alone, I wrote three books about the presidential campaign. One was called *Red November*, and recounted the Democratic Party presidential primary, where each candidate vied desperately to appear more radical than the others. A second book, *The Trumpian Virtues*, sought to distill the essence of Trump's political legacy. A third, *Neither Free Nor Fair*, discussed the deep flaws in the 2020 election.

So I have enough of a background in Trump, his politics, and his opponents to write with some expertise about what his agenda could be, or ought to be. But I did so as a journalist, and not as a campaign operative. I would describe myself as a Trump supporter, but I have also been a critic, at times. I do not agree with everything Trump has done or might want to do. This book is therefore not just a reflection of Trump's priorities but a suggestion as to what they should be.

A few caveats are in order. First, the book focuses on actions that Trump could take as president, without necessarily depending on cooperation from Congress. As

Trump learned during his first term, Congress is never sure to help—even when the president's party controls both houses, and especially when Republicans are in charge. (Democrats tend to march in lockstep; Republicans have more ideological diversity and enjoy infighting a little too much.)

Second, there are some cases in which my views differ from the president's views. For example, I am inclined to support a ban on Chinese-owned TikTok, because I do not believe that First Amendment protections apply to what is essentially enemy propaganda. But Trump opposes a ban because he believes it would help Facebook, run by Mark Zuckerberg, who spent hundreds of millions of dollars to beat Trump in 2020. So I left a TikTok ban off the presidential agenda.

I also disagree with Trump on entitlement reform. Trump has run on promises not to touch Social Security and Medicare—promises that he has kept. But these entitlement programs are in serious financial trouble and there is an urgent need for reform. So I suggested some reforms while leaving out raising the retirement age, which Trump has explicitly opposed in the past. Trump will need legislative help, anyway, to make some of the changes that are needed.

Finally, I should note that I tend to use ordinary language in describing the Trump agenda. I do not generally specify whether he would use executive orders, or executive actions, or memos. Translating some of these suggestions into action will require the expertise of an administrative law expert or a White House staff secretary. What I can say is that they are active steps—not simply "calls" for some other branch of government to do what the executive alone cannot.

The agenda is ambitious—as well it should be. It is not a "wish list" of policies, but rather a program of action. I have designed it that way because Trump will have an unusually strong mandate for sweeping change. After facing such unprecedented opposition—demonization by the media, an impeachment trial after leaving office, four prosecutions, a staggering civil lawsuit—a victorious Trump will be motivated to punish his many persecutors and have the right to do so.

But that energy needs to be channeled, beyond personal revenge and into specific actions. The opposition can be expected to challenge all of them in court—forum-shopping in the friendliest liberal jurisdictions, seeking nationwide injunctions that stop the Trump train in its tracks. Trump must anticipate that by overwhelming the left with the sheer number and speed of his actions. They will still file lawsuits, but they will have to strain their budgets and personnel to do so.

So, on the one hand, the Trump conviction in New York, absurd though it appears, is a low point in American history. On the other hand, it may signal the imminent arrival of the most exciting period of reform in the past century. A victorious Trump will have completed the greatest political comeback in American history and will have the opportunity—however briefly—to make the kinds of big changes that come along once in a generation, or perhaps several generations.

Writing this book has helped me pull myself out of the post-conviction gloom and has made me far more optimistic about what awaits America, in the election and beyond. I hope that as you consider the suggestions offered in *The Agenda*, you will absorb some of that spirit of determination and hope. Please find me online (@joelpollak on X / Twitter, for example) and share criticisms and ideas. Together, we can make what happens next worth all of the struggles that have led to it.

# Introduction

It's 10:53 p.m. on a Saturday night. Just over forty-eight hours ago, a jury of seven men and five women in Manhattan, New York, convicted former President Donald Trump of thirty-four felony counts of falsifying business records relating to payments he made to an adult film star, via his lawyer, as part of a legal non-disclosure agreement. The prosecutor, Alvin Bragg, argued in state court that Trump violated federal campaign law in failing to report these payments as campaign expenses.

Democrats are cheering the verdict. *Finally*, they believe, they will see Trump in an orange jumpsuit, headed to prison—perhaps for the rest of his life, given the potential sentences for each count. *Finally*, they believe, they can exorcise the humiliation their party incurred at Hillary Clinton's shocking defeat in the 2016 election—a loss that was compounded by the surprising success of Trump's presidency. *Finally*, they believe, they will guarantee President Joe Biden's re-election, despite his bad polls.

Republicans are angry. They donated a record $52 million to the Trump campaign in the hours after his conviction. They are hoisting upside-down American flags—the symbol of distress—and sharing them on social media. They are being joined by many ordinary Americans who may not have wanted to vote for Trump, much less to donate to him, but who are outraged that our country has been turned into a Third World banana republic by a partisan prosecutor and judge.

Bragg ran for office promising to prosecute Trump— for what, he did not say. The judge, Juan Merchan, had donated to an anti-Trump group; his daughter is a Democratic Party consultant. He allowed Bragg to bypass the statute of limitations on the crime—normally a misdemeanor—by claiming that Trump violated the law to cover up federal crimes. He did not require Bragg to state what those federal crimes were; never mind that Trump had not been convicted of any.

At trial, Judge Merchan prevented the defense from introducing evidence and calling witnesses who could have explained that Trump had not, in fact, violated federal campaign finance rules. He allowed salacious and prejudicial testimony about Trump's alleged affair. The prosecution's sole witness was a convicted liar who admitted on the stand he had stolen tens of thousands of dollars from Trump and had been trying to destroy him for years. Yet the jury found Trump guilty.

There is every reason to believe that Trump will emerge from this miscarriage of justice stronger than before. His supporters are more highly motivated than ever to help him win in November. And for the first time, as cartoonist-turned-pundit Scott Adams pointed out, Trump has earned the empathy of millions of people, many of whom once saw him as a bully posting mean tweets. If he is sentenced to prison, he can still run for president—and he may be more likely to win.

But as I sit here on a Saturday night, staring into my coffee with a feeling of unusually strong melancholy, I feel that it is not enough to wait and hope for eventual political retribution. Trump doesn't just need to win; he needs a plan to govern. And that plan needs to go beyond revenge—though certainly his tormentors have earned whatever turnabout is coming. Trump needs to draw on the pain of this moment to motivate an ambitious agenda for his first 100 days in office.

That agenda has to be decisive and comprehensive. It needs to focus on executive actions, without relying on a Congress that proved unreliable in Trump's first term, even when both houses were in Republican hands. It needs to obey the Constitution—as Biden's executive actions often have not—but it also needs to be bold. Most of all, it needs to be transformative: Trump will have the greatest mandate for sweeping change since the American Revolution.

Why does this verdict move me so? There are many reasons. One is that I come from a country where the justice system has been corrupted by politics. I was born in South Africa in 1977, and my parents believed they had to emigrate because, as my father puts it, "Illegality had become the law." Though the judiciary retained some independence, the apartheid regime interfered with it enough to ensure black voters were disenfranchised and segregation was the law of the land.

I grew up in the Chicago suburbs, and went to Harvard, but returned to South Africa in the post-apartheid era to pursue my graduate studies. I stayed on to work as a freelance journalist and political speechwriter for the leading opposition party, the Democratic Alliance (DA). I saw how the African National Congress (ANC), the party that freed South Africa from apartheid, abused its power and even used the intelligence services to suppress dissent within the government.

In many parts of the Third World, it is routine to see the judicial system abused to suppress the political opposition. Likewise, under communism, where even loyal members of the ruling party who fall out of favor suddenly find themselves in the dock. Post-communist Russia, under Vladimir Putin's tyranny, still works that way. As a heckler at Speaker's Corner in Hyde Park, in London, once put it, they believe in a two-party system: one party in power, the other in jail.

Of course, no one is above the law, as Democrats have reminded us for years. But no one is below it, either. And while a president or presidential candidate should not expect to commit crimes with impunity, none of the charges Trump faces in his four prosecutions—two state, two federal—seems credible. His opponents—Clinton in 2016, Biden in 2020—have escaped punishment for similar or worse conduct, exposing the corruption in our justice system.

It is crushing to think that this country, which is the world's oldest existing democracy, and sets the standard for the rest of the free world, could descend into the arbitrary abuse of justice that marks banana republics and failed states. My parents gave up lives of relative privilege in South Africa because they cherished the rule of law, which the United States exemplified. They knew that without justice, no society can survive. It was a lesson I learned again in South Africa.

I had been a left-wing activist in college, and a member of the College Democrats, but when I returned to Harvard to pursue a law degree, I had acquired a new skepticism that eventually led me to become a conservative Republican. I ran, unsuccessfully, for Congress in my hometown, but befriended conservative media pioneer Andrew Breitbart along the way. He hired me to join his fledgling news organization in Los Angeles, where I have worked for the past thirteen years.

I hold no particular brief for Trump. I came to admire him and his policies, about which I have written several books, but I have never been shy about criticizing him when I believe he has gone wrong. I have never been invited to Mar-a-Lago, Trump's Florida estate, where he has surrounded himself with loyalists. I would be willing, in theory, to serve in his administration, but I was not offered a post in the last administration, and I have no reason to expect I will be offered one in the next.

I am writing this book solely because I believe I can help. When Trump took office the first time, he came to the White House with a skeleton crew. Republicans in Congress were unprepared. But Democrats, and their so-called "Resistance," were ready to block anything he tried to do. They colluded with the media and the "Deep State"—the semi-permanent civil service—to undermine him at every turn. This time, Trump and his supporters must be ready on Day One.

☆    ☆    ☆

When Trump first took office in 2017, he stumbled out of the gate. After a blistering Inaugural Address in which the new president declared that "we are transferring power from Washington, DC and giving it back to you, the American People," Trump wasted several days on petty fights and personnel battles. His press secretary,

Sean Spicer, emerged in the White House briefing room after the Inauguration to complain about the media's reports of a small crowd on the National Mall.

I remember watching in dismay from my hotel room in northwest DC, where I had split a room with two friends. It had been nearly impossible to find a place to stay—not because so many people had come to see Trump take the oath of office, but because Hillary Clinton's fans had kept their bookings after she lost and showed up for the Women's March on the day after the Inauguration. They flooded the streets; they took over the city; they knew what they were doing.

There was to be no "honeymoon" for the new administration, which found itself under attack from every side at the outset. His many opponents—at the highest level, including outgoing President Barack Obama—were determined to prevent him from governing, and wanted him ousted as soon as possible and by any means necessary. Already, the intelligence services had been eavesdropping on his staff, including incoming National Security Advisor Michael Flynn.

That spying effort would later be used to frame Flynn for so-called "Russia collusion." Indeed, as Trump staff were still moving into the White House, then-FBI Director James Comey would visit Flynn for what was described as a friendly chat and what later became the FBI's basis for destroying Flynn's career. Comey also approached Trump with salacious claims about his supposed adventures in Russia from the infamous "dossier," paid for by the Clinton campaign.

All of that emerged later. At the time, I remember thinking that Trump had missed the chance to reach out to the other side—to find common ground with Democrats, to reassure them that he would govern with the best interests of the nation in mind and end the hysteria about his rise to power. Trump did win a few plaudits from Democratic leaders when he talked about spending on infrastructure, and he surprised union leaders by inviting them to tour the Oval Office with him.

Then, after just a week in office, Trump shocked the nation by introducing a sudden "travel ban" that applied to several countries—all of which, at the time, happened to be Muslim states. All were countries that were prone to terror, and which did not have the capacity to vet travelers to the United States. Later, the list would be expanded to several non-Muslim countries as well, such as North Korea. But to Democrats, this was the so-called "Muslim ban" they had dreaded.

Immediately, crowds of protesters began descending on airports, blocking traffic and adding to the confusion of officials who struggled to implement the new restrictions. Democrat officials joined the demonstrations, which formed the basis of what would be called the "Resistance." Though some Trump officials welcomed the chaos, thinking it would show Americans just how radical the opposition had become, it actually slowed down Trump's ability to implement his policies.

By 2025, circumstances will have changed. Compromise will not be a priority. If anything, Trump needs to act swiftly to identify and punish those who have abused their power to target him and his followers. There will also be opportunities for magnanimity and reconciliation. But above all, Trump needs to start his second term with a clear agenda and a plan of action, not simply to act without forethought and allow his radical opponents and their reactions to define the political terrain.

☆ ☆ ☆

All of the forces arrayed against Trump on January 20, 2017, will be there again on January 20, 2025. But he will face an additional obstacle: the fact that he will be a "lame duck" president on his first day in office. Despite jokes and memes about being president for the rest of his life, Trump will only have four years in office. Conservatives have rallied to his side but will depart just as quickly if he does anything that actually resembles an attempt to bypass the Constitution.

From the moment he returns to the White House, the political class will already be speculating about his successor. That will tend to shift the political initiative away from the Oval Office and back toward the media and the opposition—including a phalanx of Republican contenders. The Senate is likely to be Republican, given the sheer numbers of Democrats facing reelection in 2024, but the House may be in the Democrats' hands, leaving Trump facing a divided legislature.

Therefore, it is necessary for President Trump 2.0 to have a clear set of executive orders and actions ready to sign from the moment he sits down at the *Resolute* desk. He needs a plan for his first 100 days in office that is even more ambitious and decisive than the first 100 days of Franklin Delano Roosevelt's new administration during the Depression—the transformative presidency that established the "first 100 days" as a benchmark for presidential achievement.

The country is in a state of crisis. Our southern border is a disaster, with millions of migrants arriving from around the world, paying tens of thousands of dollars each to cartels and entering the United States with virtual impunity. Our inner cities are empty hellscapes of homelessness and crime, with many urban centers still struggling to recover from the pandemic and from the reduction in police funding that remains the legacy of the "Black Lives Matter" riots of 2020.

Our schools are struggling, beset by radical agendas determined to indoctrinate children with political agendas on race and transgenderism rather than to prepare them with the basic math and reading skills they need to compete in a changing economy. Our national debt is exploding, as the emergency spending of the COVID-19 era has become institutionalized, with trillions spent on "infrastructure" like electric vehicle charging stations that somehow are never built.

The inflation rate has stabilized somewhat, but remains high, with interest rates at prohibitively high levels that make home ownership a distant dream for many young Americans. The middle class can no longer afford a middle-class lifestyle—at least not in the cities where the best job opportunities are. The birth rate has collapsed over the past twenty years, thanks to the soaring costs of childcare and to a culture overtaken by smartphones instead of human interactions.

Abroad, America's enemies are on the march. China is spreading its influence in the Pacific and around the world. Russia, having invaded Ukraine on Biden's watch, is consolidating its gains. And a nuclear Iran looms, enriched by untold billions of dollars in sanctions relief from the Biden administration, and emboldened by the brutal success that its terrorist proxies have enjoyed in attacking Israel and stopping shipping through the Red Sea. Our national security is at stake.

Worst of all, the country has lost faith in itself. Trump promised to "Make America Great Again" but was told by Democrats that America "was never that great." We have become consumed by our country's flaws rather than focusing on its many triumphs and its limitless potential. Trump is a divisive figure, but he is also one of the few leaders bold enough to take the actions necessary to restore America's confidence. In the pages that follow, I offer an agenda to do exactly that.

# Chapter 1

# The Rule of Law

## Grant Pardons and Commutations

Donald Trump's first order of business must be to restore confidence in the rule of law. For nearly a decade, he and his supporters have been the targets of an unprecedented and unfair campaign of legal persecution that has undermined public faith in the justice system. For that reason, he must make sweeping changes on his first day back in the Oval Office that right the many wrongs perpetrated against Trump supporters. He should begin with several pardons.

**1. Pardon all non-violent January 6 offenders.** Hundreds of people have been prosecuted and jailed for non-violent offenses related to the Capitol riot of January 6, 2021. Often, they simply walked onto the Capitol grounds or through doors opened by Capitol Police. They were smeared in the media and tried in a hostile jurisdiction, and often lacked access to exculpatory evidence. Trump should immediately pardon all non-violent defendants—including himself.

**2. Pardon those accused of contempt of Congress for defying the January 6 Committee.** Several Trump aides were held in contempt of Congress, and two—Stephen K. Bannon and Peter Navarro—were prosecuted for it. But the aides had raised legitimate issues of executive privilege. Moreover, the committee defied precedent by rejecting the minority party's chosen representatives, rendering subsequent subpoenas invalid under the enabling House legislation.

**3. Pardon all those accused of federal crimes in relation to the "documents" case.** President Trump and several aides face charges over their handling of presidential documents that he had legal reason to believe were his personal property, and whose disposition should have been handled through negotiation, not prosecution—and certainly not with an invasive search, guns drawn, at the private home of a former president. He should pardon all involved.

**4. Pardon all accused, including himself, on state charges in New York and Georgia.** There are constitutional questions about whether a president can issue pardons for state crimes. Yet since the state prosecutions against him in New York, and against him and others in Georgia, depend on the enforcement of federal election law, Trump arguably has authority. He should issue the pardons regardless and let state prosecutors try to challenge them in court.

**5. Pardon pro-life activists prosecuted by the Biden administration.** The Department of Justice has targeted pro-life activists for protesting at abortion clinics, while often ignoring attacks by pro-abortion radicals against pro-life pregnancy centers. The prosecutions of pro-life activists have been ideologically motivated and have led to excessive sentences against non-violent individuals. President Trump will immediately pardon imprisoned pro-life activists.

**6. Pardon meme-maker Douglass Mackey.** Mackey was sentenced to federal prison in 2023 for posting jokes online that federal prosecutors claimed were efforts to mislead Hillary Clinton voters into not casting their ballots. The case punished what would be, in any other context, an attempt at humor and parody. Mackey was targeted only because Democrats were looking for scapegoats for their loss in 2016. He is one of many who suffered unjustly for their vendetta.

**7. Commute Ross Ulbricht's sentence.** The founder of the Silk Road online marketplace, which has been used for drug deals and other contraband activities, is currently serving two life sentences—a vastly excessive punishment. Without pardoning him—because his activities did, in fact, cause harm to people indirectly—President Trump should commute his sentence. Again, the federal legal authorities who pursued him have lost the presumption of good faith.

## Launch Investigations

For years, Democratic Party operatives have coordinated their efforts to target Trump and his supporters through connections and mechanisms that have never fully been understood. The party has been aided by loyalists in the federal civil service; in intelligence agencies; in federal law enforcement; in the media; in academia; and in the non-profit sector. This left-wing shadow government must be fully exposed through investigations because it is a threat to democracy.

**1. Appoint a Special Counsel to investigate the Democratic Party.** The Democratic Party no longer operates as an ordinary political party, but as a criminal enterprise, a secondary state that controls politics both inside and outside of government. Just as the January 6 Committee and various investigations of Trump supporters provided Democrats with a trove of information about how Republican politics functions internally, a Special Counsel should expose the left.

**2. Release the name of the so-called "whistleblower" in the first impeachment.** The public never learned the identity of the "whistleblower" who targeted Trump over his phone call with the president of Ukraine, plunging the nation into chaos. Then–House Intelligence Committee chair Rep. Adam Schiff (D-CA) promised to produce the whistleblower for testimony but reneged. The whistleblower should be named and called to testify to Congress about his role in the affair.

**3. Appoint a Special Counsel to investigate Adam Schiff.** Schiff was already booted off the Intelligence Committee for lying to the public about information to which only he had access, misleading Americans about "Russian collusion" and other matters. But Schiff also violated the civil liberties of witnesses called to his committees, and even spied on fellow members and the president's lawyers. Schiff must be investigated for crimes committed in the pursuit of Trump.

**4. Direct the Department of Justice Civil Rights Division to investigate antisemitism on campus.** The Civil Rights Division has been silent about the violence and antisemitism at elite universities, which is thought to receive funding from foreign sources—including some that have possible links to terrorism. The campus unrest, which has spilled over into the streets of many American cities, is an attempt to disrupt American life and indoctrinate future leaders.

**5. Appoint a Special Counsel to investigate the Democrats' "shadow campaign" of 2020.** Democrats have prosecuted Trump supporters for casting doubt on the 2020 election, but *Time* magazine published a proud confession in 2021 that Democrats had run a "shadow campaign" to ensure victory by creating a sense of panic around the coronavirus pandemic, force universal vote-by-mail, and suppress information that might embarrass Joe Biden. An inquiry is overdue.

**6. Appoint a Special Counsel to investigate the January 6 Committee.** From the destruction of documents, including thousands of pages of evidence and recordings of witness testimony, to the abuse of the due process rights of witnesses, the January 6 Committee was a Stalinist show trial that appeared to break several laws. An investigation is needed into the members of that committee and the lawyers and staff who worked on it in an effort to subvert democracy.

**7. Launch IRS investigations of left-wing non-profits that abuse their status for political purposes.** Groups like Media Matters, which do little except suppress crit-ics of the Democratic Party, are formally recognized as charities under Section 501(c)3 of the tax code. Yet they are abusing that tax-exempt status to raise money for what are essentially political purposes. The IRS must be directed to probe the activities of these groups and pun-ish them, if necessary.

## Reform Agencies

The law enforcement, national security, and intelligence agencies of this country have been exposed as parti-san institutions. While many of the rank-and-file are patriots doing their best for the country, the leaders of these agencies have either enlisted directly in the effort to undermine Trump, or have remained silent as oth-ers have done so. Prosecutors, at every level, have been corrupted by the same political forces. Trump therefore needs to make urgent agency reforms.

**1. Fire the entire senior leadership of the DOJ, FBI, CIA, and NSA.** All of them must go. The fact that senior DOJ and FBI officials keep joining anti-Trump initiatives; and that fifty-one former intelligence and national security officials signed onto a letter in 2020 falsely claiming that the infamous Hunter Biden laptop was Russian disin-formation; suggests that these agencies must be totally rebuilt. Qualified officials can reapply for their jobs. All of them must be re-vetted.

**2. Fire every single US Attorney.** This mass turnover of federal prosecutors is by now routine, but should be immediate and sweeping on the first day of the new administration. The entire federal prosecution service needs to be renewed and must be staffed by people who are committed to the rule of law, not to prosecuting political opponents—or offering sweetheart plea deals to those politicians whom they wish to protect for their own partisan reasons.

**3. Suspend federal funding to any local prosecutors who refuse to enforce the law.** The president is limited by the Impoundment Control Act in his ability to withhold spending that Congress has expressly authorized. But because George Soros–funded prosecutors around the country are refusing to prosecute criminals or to seek harsh sentences for violent crimes, cities have become unlivable and federal money is being wasted. Let local DAs sue if they object.

**4. End all consent decrees to supervise local police departments.** The Obama and Biden administrations attempted to restrict law enforcement at the local level by supervising police departments—even, and especially, in Democrat-run cities—for supposed brutality. As this supervision has increased, crime has often increased as well. The DOJ should stop trying to hold back local law enforcement, and allow the cops on the beat to do their jobs properly.

**5. Order a DOJ investigation into "lawfare" and blacklist anyone involved.** Trump's opponents have used what they call "lawfare" to pursue civil and criminal cases against him with the specific goal of destroying his political career, and destroying him personally. The DOJ should track down every attorney and activist involved in that effort, and blacklist them from ever working again for the federal justice system, which they have already abused for partisan gain.

**6. Revoke the security clearance of every one of the fifty-one officials who signed the Hunter Biden letter.** Fifty-one former senior national security and intelligence officials signed a misleading public letter in October 2020 that falsely claimed the story of Hunter Biden's wayward laptop—with evidence of Joe Biden's corruption—was Russian "disinformation." Their claims helped sway the election toward Biden. Their security clearance should be immediately revoked.

**7. Order reviews of asset forfeiture policies and FISA warrant applications.** The DOJ has a policy of asset forfeiture, under which the assets of accused criminals are often seized by the government prior to any finding of guilt. That policy should be reviewed, as should the DOJ's process for interacting with the Foreign Intelligence Surveillance Act courts, which was abused when the DOJ attempted to spy on the Trump campaign and administration in 2016–2017.

## Fight Crime and Drugs

We have also witnessed the collapse of the rule of law more generally with the reluctance, or refusal, of national and municipal authorities to enforce existing laws. Part of the problem is the broader issue of border security (see Chapter 2). And part of it is a liberal approach to crime, homelessness, drugs, and other problems that have made many of America's great cities unlivable and that have devastated rural communities. We must save our communities—now.

**1. Direct federal prosecutors to seek the maximum possible sentences for large-scale drug dealers, including death.** Those who deal in highly addictive and deadly substances like fentanyl, which kill tens of thousands of Americans every year, should face the maximum penalty as a deterrent. We need to address the problem of supply in China and at the southern border, but we also need to end the mechanism of distribution throughout the United States.

**2. Expand the national public health emergency around fentanyl and opioids.** The first Trump administration declared the opioid pandemic a national public health emergency. That needs to be expanded and focused on the spread of fentanyl, which often finds its way into the supply chain through other drugs marketed as off-market medicines and leads unsuspecting users to overdose. The White House must become a bully pulpit for awareness of fentanyl.

**3. Direct the Federal Emergency Management Agency (FEMA) to address the disaster of homelessness.** Homelessness cannot be solved by buying hotel rooms or building tiny homes. Many homeless people are mentally ill; some are addicted to drugs; some refuse to move indoors. FEMA needs to set up emergency triage operations that will move the homeless off the streets and direct them to services appropriate to their needs, including involuntary commitment.

**4. Surge federal law enforcement to cities experiencing violent crime waves.** Just as the first Trump administration did during Operation Legend, the second Trump administration should surge federal law enforcement officers and resources to cities that are experiencing waves of violent crime. These include cities like San Francisco and New York, where shoplifting has gutted retail in once-popular shopping districts and people are constant targets of petty crime.

**5. Federalize the National Guard in jurisdictions that practice "sanctuary" policies on immigration.** The previous Trump administration attempted to deny certain federal funds to cities that refused to cooperate with immigration authorities. These efforts were challenged in court. But there is another approach: the president, as commander-in-chief, can federalize the National Guard in "sanctuary" states and use it to enforce immigration law at the local level.

**6. Direct that federal funding for local police be set aside for school police forces.** Far-left unions in cities like Los Angeles have defunded school police forces that have kept children safe. Federal funding for local law enforcement should be earmarked specifically for local police forces that protect schools from gangs, drugs, crime, and the threat of mass shootings, which target schools that are known "gun-free zones" and that lack their own armed security guards.

**7. Appoint a Special Counsel to investigate the problem of corruption in city government.** Too many of our cities are run as one-party states, where corruption has become the ordinary course of business as Democrats are able to enrich themselves and their cronies. Though the federal government prosecutes individual cases of corruption, a comprehensive approach is needed to find the weaknesses in our system of municipal government and to root them out.

# Chapter 2

# The Border

## Secure the Border

The crisis at the southern border is the greatest national security crisis in the post–Cold War era, and it is entirely the result of choices made by the Biden administration to undo effective policies that had been in place at the end of the Trump administration. The motives may be political, in that Democrats hope to convert migrants into votes; they may be economic, in that big business likes cheap labor. But the effect on our country is corrosive. We need border security, now.

**1. Close the southern border to migration completely, including legal immigration.** No migrant who appears at the southern border, whether at a point of entry or elsewhere, will be admitted into the United States. All will be processed and deported, regardless of work permits, asylum claims, family reunification, or other reasons. Legal migration can only be continued in a safe and orderly manner when the situation at the southern border has stabilized.

**2. Reinstate the "Remain in Mexico" policy.** Under President Trump, the US adopted the policy, consistent with international law, that asylum-seekers must claim refuge in the first safe country that they enter—which, in this case, would be Mexico. Those who wish to file asylum claims—when the border reopens to them—will not be allowed to enter the US and remain, pending their court date, but rather will be required to remain in Mexico until that date arrives.

**3. Build the wall.** The Biden administration halted construction of the border wall, wasting billions of dollars as construction materials were left to rust. The Trump administration will immediately resume construction of the wall, using funds from the national security budget until and unless Congress allocates additional funding. Where a wall is not topographically feasible, the administration will deploy both human and electronic resources to prevent illegal entries.

**4. End "catch-and-release."** Migrants have been turning themselves in to Border Patrol, knowing that after they are processed and told to appear at a distant court date, they will be allowed to remain in the United States. The Trump administration will take executive action to end this policy immediately. All migrants who are apprehended will be deported to their countries of origin or escorted to the Mexican side of the border to await their court dates.

**5. Demand that Mexico stop the caravans and the cartels.** Under pressure from President Trump, Mexico had deployed thousands of soldiers along its southern border to intercept migrant caravans from Central America. President Biden abandoned that agreement, but President Trump will demand its restoration. President Trump will also demand that Mexico take action to break up the human smuggling cartels that bring millions of people to the border.

**6. Sanction countries sending illegal migrants to the United States.** The countries of origin of the migrants are no longer just the "Northern Triangle" nations of Guatemala, El Salvador, and Honduras. Many are traveling from Asia and Africa, boarding flights without proper entry documents and then making their way northward to the border. The Trump administration will announce sanctions on any country that knowingly allows citizens to leave illegally for the US.

**7. Federalize the National Guard in border states to assist Border Patrol.** California, among other border states, has participated in operations along the southern border—though never to enforce the border itself. Given the reluctance of some states to participate in enforcement, the president should federalize the National Guard to help the border until the wall can be built and until the Border Patrol can handle the job of keeping out or deterring illegal migrants on its own.

## Close Loopholes

It is commonly accepted that the American immigration system is "broken." However, it is working exactly as Democrats intend: to maximize the number of illegal migrants. In the legal immigration system, our laws prioritize family reunification over skills, creating a growing foreign-born population that is less likely to appreciate the specific values that America represents and the opportunities it provides. We need urgent immigration reforms.

**1. Suspend the immigration "parole" system.** The Biden administration has used the "parole" system to allow millions of migrants to stay in the country without fear of deportation. Excessive parole has created the expectation that these migrants will be granted a form of legal permanent residence, adding incentives for more migrants to risk the journey. The new administration should issue an executive order suspending new grants of "parole" until the border is secure.

**2. Immediately end renewals of the Deferred Action for Childhood Arrivals (DACA) program.** In 2018, President Trump offered Democrats a pathway to citizenship for 1.8 million people who were brought to the US as minors—the so-called "Dreamers"—but Democrats refused to take the deal. The DACA program is unconstitutional and incentivizes continued efforts to migrate to the country illegally—and to traffic children to do so. It must be suspended.

**3. End "chain migration" through executive action.** Democrats in Congress refused to accept Trump's offer to "Dreamers," partly because he demanded an end to chain migration, among other changes. But as president, he has broad authority over immigration, and could direct the US Citizenship and Immigration Services (USCIS) simply to stop processing any applications for family migration that are not also qualified under some other category.

**4. End Temporary Protected Status (TPS) for most, if not all, foreign groups.** The US has been generous to a fault in extending TPS to migrants from countries that have experienced internal conflict or natural disasters.

We cannot, however, be a release valve for all of the world's problems. Moreover, what is "temporary" to begin with is treated, over time, as a form of permanent legal status. An executive order should be used to wind down TPS for most cases.

**5. Immediately restore the use of the word "alien" in federal documents.** The term "alien" is not offensive and has been used for centuries to describe people from abroad. Democrats have tried to change the language that Americans use to describe immigrants, both legal and illegal, in the hope that doing so would help reduce opposition to their radical policies. President Trump should direct that federal agencies return to the standard language that was used prior to 2021.

**6. Restrict federal transportation funds from states granting driver's licenses to illegal aliens.** There is ample precedent for the use of federal transportation funds to enforce federal policy, such as a national drinking age of twenty-one. Issuing driver's licenses to illegal aliens creates the illusion of permanent status. It also increases the risk that foreigners would register to vote through automatic "motor voter" programs, which has happened in previous elections in states like California.

**7. Prohibit illegal aliens from benefiting directly from federal programs such as student loan relief.** It is difficult, legally and morally, to restrict federal funding from services that benefit illegal aliens in a general sense, such as health and education systems. But the government can ensure that those who are in the country illegally do not receive federal housing assistance, student loan relief, and other funds whose benefits are primarily intended to go to Americans.

## Boost Internal Enforcement

It is important to recognize that the Biden administration did more than end the Trump administration's effective border policies. Biden allowed millions of migrants into the country—millions who, Democrats appear to believe, will one day become voters. At the very least, they will change the apportionment of congressional seats to counteract the migration away from "blue" states. President Trump must act to undo what was an attack on American democracy.

**1. Direct the US Census to distinguish between citizens, legal residents, and illegal aliens.** The first Trump administration attempted to implement this policy, but did so too late, and lost in the Supreme Court on administrative law grounds (one of the few cases in which Trump lost on constitutional grounds, despite the Democrats' rhetoric about his authoritarian behavior). Trump should ensure the census makes distinctions so that Congress can act accordingly.

**2. Add immigration status to federal forms for a wide variety of purposes.** Even if the data collected is not going to be used for any particular purpose other than information, the federal government should collect data on the illegal alien population, which was once said to be 11 million people strong, but whose true size "in the shadows" is unknown. Asking about immigration status—on penalty of perjury—could also be a deterrent against illegal migration.

**3. Deny any form of permanent residency or citizenship to anyone who entered the US unlawfully after January 20, 2021.** The Biden policy was not only irresponsible, but also prejudicial, in that it changed America's demographic and political reality in ways that were illegitimate. Democrats stalled for years and claimed, falsely, that the border was secure. They cannot be allowed to benefit from that; none of those migrants should ever have legal status.

**4. Direct the Department of Justice to conduct a review of safeguards against foreign voting.** It is a fact that some foreigners have been added to voter rolls—whether on purpose or inadvertently—and each foreign vote cast dilutes the vote of an American citizen. The Department of Justice should investigate the phenomenon of foreign registration and voting, and evaluate safeguards in every state, making recommendations or legal filings as necessary.

**5. Restore the "zero tolerance" policy against abuse of children.** This policy was ended after Democrats claimed it led to "kids in cages." In reality, adults and children were temporarily separated at the border to verify their relation to one another, in order to prevent abuse and trafficking; the "cages" were fence partitions built by the Obama administration. Children should never be used as passports into America. An executive order should reimpose the tough policy.

**6. Empower Immigration and Customs Enforcement (ICE) to pursue migrants.** Under the Trump administration, ICE prioritized hardened criminals who were in the country illegally. Given the new and urgent circumstances, in which millions of people have entered the US in the past few years alone, it is urgent to pursue them and deport them, with the goal of returning to the *status quo ante* prior to 2021. Biden's illegal immigration must be undone as far as possible.

**7. Offer federal support for state efforts to bus migrants to liberal jurisdictions.** Texas and Florida have made a point of relocating illegal migrants to "blue" states and cities that support the "sanctuary" policies that have made a mess of the border. The federal government, too, moves migrants from the border—to communities throughout America. President Trump should take executive action to ensure migrants are moved to places that support them—from afar.

## Reform Immigration

While barring illegal immigration, as well as closing down methods of legal immigration that are often abused, the US should also develop a narrower and more effective policy of legal immigration that prioritizes skills and service. As President Trump has often been fond of saying, even when building a wall along the southern border, we should also build a "big, beautiful door" for the most deserving, ambitious, and law-abiding legal immigrants to make America their home.

**1. Direct USCIS to develop a new application process that prioritizes skills.** When legal immigration is opened more broadly again—once there is border security—it should place highest priority on immigrants with skills that the US economy needs and values. President Trump should issue an executive order to the agency directing that it identify the best ways to create a skills-based immigration system, and make appropriate legislative recommendations.

**2. Allow student visas in science, technology, engineering, and mathematics (STEM) to be converted into permanent residency.** The US trains the world's best and brightest at our universities—and then they leave, taking skills, knowledge, and valuable research experience back with them. A significant portion of foreign STEM students would prefer to stay in the US. We should offer them ways to do so, and benefit as a society from their skills and innovations.

**3. Focus asylum only on the most deserving refugees and those best able to assimilate, especially persecuted Christians.** Asylum is for desperate people facing religious and political persecution, not for people who simply want to earn higher wages and send remittances back home. The president also has the power to prioritize Christian refugees who are persecuted—such as in China, Nigeria, or the Caucasus region—solely due to their religious beliefs.

**4. Screen out immigrants who hold extreme anti-Israel views.** Germany has already begun excluding any immigrants who do not believe Israel has the right to exist. These migrants are generally radical Muslims who have been at the heart of extremist anti-Israel and antisemitic riots in Germany and elsewhere in Europe. Just as the US bars communists from being given permanent residency, it should bar those who hate Israel, a key ally, from entering the US.

**5. Create an educational training program to drill immigrants in English and American civics.** Some countries, like Israel, require all new immigrants to graduate from immersion programs that teach them the local language, customs, history, and traditions. The US waits until the citizenship test to demand that immigrants learn basic civics lessons. All would-be legal immigrants should have a crash course in American civics and values *before* they are approved.

**6. End programs through which the Department of Homeland Security flies migrants directly to the US.** The Biden administration has turned the US into a smuggling cartel, in effect, appealing to would-be illegal migrants to board American planes rather than trying to walk across the border. No one will pass through the "big, beautiful door" of legal immigration if the alternative is so comfortable, so heavily subsidized, and so without consequences.

**7. Educate would-be immigrants about the legal immigration process.** Many migrants who cross the southern border after paying thousands of dollars to cartels do not actually know that there is a legal way to apply for entry and permanent residency to the US—a way that is often less expensive. Instead of advertising US welfare programs, as the Obama administration did in migrant-prone countries, the US must educate and offer advice on how to apply for legal immigration.

Chapter 3

# Foreign Policy

## End the Ukraine War

President Trump conducted one of the most successful foreign policies of any president in US history. He was the first president in years not to start a war. He crafted the Abraham Accords, the first peace deal in the Middle East in generations. He also kept China and Russia in check, despite false claims of Russian "collusion." Biden has set the world on fire, notably in Eastern Europe and the Middle East. Trump should end the war in Ukraine in a responsible way.

**1. Convene a summit for peace talks between Russia and Ukraine.** Until now, President Biden—who famously declared "diplomacy is back" upon taking office—has avoided any diplomacy, pushing instead for an amorphous and illusory "victory" against a nuclear-armed power. Billions of dollars and hundreds of thousands of lives have been wasted for a stalemate. President Trump should immediately convene peace talks to bring an end to the conflict.

**2. Appoint an inspector general for Ukraine military funding.** Unlike the war in Afghanistan, there has been no inspector general to trace funding in the Ukraine war. Ukraine is known to be one of the most corrupt countries in Europe, and there are legitimate concerns that money sent for its defense is being siphoned off by corrupt politicians. Before billions of dollars are sent to Ukraine for reconstruction, taxpayers need to know how the money sent thus far has been used.

**3. Step up pressure on NATO allies to contribute their committed defense spending.** Though Trump helped boost compliance among NATO members with their commitment to spend 2 percent of their GDP on defense, and the Ukraine war has inspired even more countries to step up, many of NATO's members are still delinquent. The refusal to take collective security seriously has weakened NATO and encouraged Russia and other rivals to take full advantage.

**4. Introduce sanctions on Russia and Iran for mutual assistance in war.** Iran has been supplying Russia with drones, and Russia has been helping Iran with nuclear technologies and air defenses. Both countries are promoting instability and threatening US allies. President Trump should end the cooperative relationship between the two countries by imposing sanctions on both—sanctions that, in the case of Iran, the Biden administration has been eager to waive.

**5. Investigate Ukrainian interference in American politics.** Russian interference has been the target of many investigations and prosecutions. But Ukrainian actors who have interfered in US elections—going back to Ukraine's support for Hillary Clinton in 2016—has also been a major problem. The new Trump administration should launch an investigation of Ukrainian officials so that the public knows whom they have influenced and how they have done so.

**6. Investigate both Russia and Ukraine for war crimes.** There is evidence that Russia has deported thousands of Ukrainians, including children, to Russia in an effort to erase their national identity. Ukraine has also repressed Russian Orthodox churches. Both sides have allegedly targeted civilians and violated the laws of war. President Trump should direct the State Department to pursue an independent and impartial investigation of both sides in the war.

**7. Expand exports of liquified natural gas to Europe as an alternative to Russian energy.** President Trump tried to warn Germany and the rest of Europe about the consequences of their dependence on Russian fossil fuels. He was mocked at the time, but was proven correct by events. In the next administration, Trump should reverse Biden's restrictions on natural gas exports so that the US can displace Russia as a major energy source for western Europe.

## Defend Israel

No administration—not even Barack Obama's administration—has done as much to jeopardize the US-Israel relationship and Israel's national security as the Biden administration. It restored funding to organizations that play a role in Palestinian terror; it relieved sanctions on the Iranian regime; it publicly opposed the democratically elected Israeli government; it adopted Hamas's bargaining positions. President Trump will act to defend Israel and promote peace.

**1. Immediately restore sanctions against Iran that have been lifted or waived by the Biden administration.** The Biden administration has allowed Iran to gain access to untold billions of dollars through sanctions relief and waivers that have then been available for terrorist groups under its control. The new administration should immediately restore and enforce those sanctions and add new ones for Iran's documented role in ongoing terror around the world.

**2. Publicly support, in advance, any preemptive strike that Israel may take to stop a nuclear Iran.** When the US clearly supports Israel, Iran and its terrorist militias tend to stand down. The new Trump administration should issue a memorandum declaring that the US will support Israel in the event that the Israeli government decides that Iran's nuclear program has reached a point of no return such that regional peace and stability requires it to be destroyed.

**3. Remove all restrictions from Israel in its fight against Iranian-backed terror groups.** The Biden administration has forced Israel to fight back against Hamas with one hand tied behind its back, threatening to withhold weapons and ammunition from Israel if it does not conduct military operations the way the White House wants it to do so. The new administration should declare that as a matter of policy, it will give Israel a free hand to do what it must to win.

**4. Permanently end funding for the United Nations Relief and Works Agency (UNRWA).** President Trump cut off funding to UNRWA because of its role in indoctrinating Palestinians to hate Israel and encourage terror.

The Biden administration restored all funding that the
Trump administration had ended. UNRWA employees
went on to cheer the October 7 terror attacks, and several have been accused of participating in them. The
funding must end now.

**5. Comply with the Taylor Force Act and stop funding
Palestinian groups.** The Taylor Force Act prevents US
taxpayer money from being spent on the Palestinian
Authority while it still subsidizes terror. The Biden
administration has tried to evade its provisions by funding groups within the Palestinian Territories. That, in
turn, has led to federal litigation. Trump should immediately end that funding and pressure the Palestinian
Authority to end its brutal policies.

**6. Pressure Arab countries to accept and resettle
Palestinian refugees.** Egypt and other US allies have
added to the suffering of Palestinians in Gaza by refusing to accept temporary refugees during the war. Many
countries do not allow Palestinian refugees from 1948
to settle, thus prolonging grievances for generations.
The Trump administration should indicate that it will
withhold foreign aid from countries that refuse to accept
Palestinian refugees and resettle them.

**7. End all sanctions on Israeli individuals and institu-
tions.** The Biden administration took the unprecedented

step of sanctioning Israelis for so-called "settler violence," punishing those who had never been accused of crimes and creating the precedent for a broader boycott. It also cut off links to universities in Israeli cities in the West Bank. All of these sanctions, which were adopted during wartime and therefore helped Hamas and Iran, should be repealed permanently.

## Downgrade the UN

The United Nations (UN) has shown itself in recent months to be an institution without the moral backbone to condemn terrorism. It has, instead, become a partner with Israel's enemies in their effort to murder innocent civilians and bring about the destruction of the Jewish state, in total disregard for the UN Charter. The UN has also nurtured anti-American sentiment while failing to act against our enemies. For example, it recently allowed Iran to lead a disarmament conference, even as the Iranian regime pursues nuclear weapons to threaten America and our allies. The US should diminish the role of the UN in our foreign policy.

**1. Demand that the UN disband the UNRWA and replace it with other agencies.** As noted above, UNRWA helps exacerbate the Israeli-Palestinian conflict. There are other organizations that provide similar functions that can be introduced into Palestinian communities in its stead. Over time, these communities—in Gaza, the West Bank, and elsewhere in the Middle East—need to be moved beyond their dependence on the UN and the largesse of international donors.

**2. Warn the UN that the US will cut off funding completely if it recognizes a Palestinian state.** The only way to resolve the Israeli-Palestinian conflict is through direct negotiations between the two parties to resolve issues like borders, a capital, and refugees. If the UN decides to reward terrorism by preempting that process, in empty gestures that would simply prolong the conflict, the US will cut off its funding to the UN, ending its ability to function.

**3. Withdraw from the UN Human Rights Council.** The Obama administration joined the Human Rights Council even though it had already become an anti-Israel and anti-American echo chamber. It failed to achieve any meaningful reforms. The Trump administration pulled out of the council, but the Biden administration entered it again, giving it undue legitimacy while barely making any meaningful changes to it. Trump should immediately leave it again.

**4. Introduce resolutions at the United Nations Security Council to condemn Hamas and Hezbollah as terrorist organizations.** It is appalling that the UN refuses to declare Hamas and Hezbollah to be terrorist organizations, and the US should press the issue. Though Russia and China are likely to veto, it is useful to have them on record—and useful to embarrass the UN, which takes high-minded moral stances but has no moral ground upon which to stand.

**5. Renew sanctions against the International Criminal Court (ICC) and its officials.** The Trump administrations slapped sanctions on the ICC and officials who wanted to investigate American soldiers and officials for supposed war crimes in the fight against terror. Trump responded by sanctioning ICC officials. The Biden administration dropped the sanctions, recognizing the bias of the ICC but promising reform. Indictments against Israel followed.

**6. Cut funding to all UN agencies that are permanently devoted to campaigning against Israel.** Many UN agencies and officials simply exist to demonize Israel and prolong the conflict. For example, UN Special Rapporteur for Human Rights in "Palestine" Francesca Albanese has repeatedly made antisemitic statements in her campaigns against Israel. The administration should demand her firing and take executive action to withhold funding from such agencies.

**7. Demand reform at the World Health Organization (WHO), which covered up for China during the coronavirus pandemic.** The WHO, a specialized agency of the UN led by Dr. Tedros Ghebreyesus, failed to transmit warnings about the new virus and insisted—when it had reason to know better—that transmission to humans was impossible, citing China. Yet the same officials remain in charge at the WHO. The US should restore Trump's ban on WHO funding until changes are made.

## Counter China

President Trump took a firm stand against China, raising tariffs on Chinese goods and building up the US military to counter growing Chinese threats in the western Pacific. President Biden came into office with a poor track record on China and a serious scandal involving his family's business interests and ties to the Chinese regime. He has done little to change the balance. President Trump would counter China's aggressive policies and restore American strength.

**1. Restore America's tough trade policy toward China.** President Biden retained most of the tariffs that President Trump had imposed on Chinese imports. He is now promising, belatedly, to protect the American electric vehicle industry by slapping new tariffs on China. But that is not enough to punish China for its predatory trade practices. President Trump should announce executive actions on his first day in office to impose new tariffs on a variety of Chinese goods.

**2. Take firm action against China on fentanyl.** The chemical components for deadly fentanyl are manufactured in China before being shipped to Central America for processing. President Trump asked China to act against known producers of these chemicals; President Biden has done even less. China has had its chance to act but did nothing. President Trump should impose strong sanctions on China and to Chinese businesses linked to those that produce fentanyl.

**3. Expand US naval presence in the western Pacific.** The US needs to return to an assertive posture in the western Pacific, sending a clear signal to China that America intends to defend its allies, including Taiwan, from aggression. Congress needs to fund the expansion of the US Navy so that it can ensure China does not surpass America's fleet. But in the meantime, the US can deploy more naval forces to the western Pacific as a sign of strength.

**4. Punish China for developing relations with Hamas and other terror groups.** China has, astonishingly, given full support to Hamas in its conflict with Israel. There are even claims that it has helped to arm the terror group.

The US should sanction all countries that provide material and political support to Hamas, but should start with China, which wants to be taken seriously as a player on the international stage but is supporting the world's most brutal terrorists.

**5. Suspend Chinese student visas to the United States.** China has abused the American education system by sending students to study at US universities who are carefully vetted in advance for political loyalty. They return to China with expertise that fuels China's industrial growth and its military expansion. The Trump administration should announce an immediate restriction on Chinese student visas—and tie further restrictions to the fight against fentanyl.

**6. Extend federal scholarships and tuition assistance for Chinese studies.** America needs to be prepared for the certainty of competition, and the possibility of conflict, with China. We need to train a generation of students who will help manage US-Chinese relations—whether peaceful or otherwise—and to do that we need more citizens who speak Mandarin and understand China. President Trump should use his authority on student loans to announce new incentives.

**7. Close loopholes in free trade agreements that are exploited by China.** Free trade deals with many developing countries have led to Chinese companies setting up shop in those places and taking advantage of the agreements without necessarily providing the intended benefits to locals. The Africa Growth and Opportunity Act (AGOA), for example, has been exploited by Chinese firms that open textile factories in Africa to take advantage of access to US markets, leading local leaders to observe that African entrepreneurs have not benefited to the same degree. President Trump should direct the State Department to review all such agreements.

# Chapter 4

# Faith

## Restore Prayer

Americans are experiencing a crisis of faith unlike any in our history. Though we are still a more religious nation than any other in the free world, church attendance has plummeted and family life has declined. We also lack faith in ourselves—as a nation, and as individuals. We are more focused on our faults, and our fears, than our potential. The second Trump administration must make faith an urgent topic of public policy and engineer a spiritual revival, starting with prayer.

**1. Begin White House functions with an invocation.** The White House does not typically begin events with a prayer, even though invocations are routine at almost every other public function in the United States—including in

Congress, where the chaplain opens each day's proceed-
ings with a prayer. The White House should have access
to clergy who can recite invocations, and should prepare
standard texts and protocols for every public occasion.

**2. Begin the White House press briefings with a moment
of reflection.** The White House press briefing is probably
the most-watched public meeting in the United States.
And yet it does not begin with a prayer. Instead, it often
begins with banter between the White House staff and
the press, symbolizing their elite familiarity. The press
secretary should begin with a short text and a moment
of reflection to set a different mood—and to set an example for the nation.

**3. Invite clergy to make regular presentations at the
White House.** The First Amendment is the basis for the
separation of church and state. But it applies principally
to Congress, not to the White House. And the White
House can invite interested clergy of every faith to share
wisdom, Bible readings, sermons, and life lessons so
that Americans can benefit and deepen their awareness
of faith. White House publications and events should
also be devoted to the purpose.

**4. Hold daily religious studies at the White House, open
to the public.** The White House facility can host daily
Bible study events, open to the public (albeit with

limited ticketing, similar to White House tours). These daily sessions will set an appropriate tone for the conduct of business in the White House and will encourage Bible study more generally throughout the country. A rotating group of clergy will be appointed on a volunteer basis to lead the sessions.

**5. Announce that a quiet moment of quiet reflection will be encouraged in schools.** The Supreme Court ruled against school prayer in 1962. But schools can still hold a moment of quiet reflection and comply with the First Amendment. The president should issue an executive order directing the Department of Education to announce that public schools across the country will be encouraged to adopt a moment of quiet reflection during which prayers may be said.

**6. Establish a commission to compose an ecumenical national prayer.** The Pledge of Allegiance is well-known to schoolchildren across the nation. Similarly, there can be a short text that is used by schools nationwide as a national prayer—one that does not endorse any particular religion, but which acknowledges a higher power. The White House should invite religious leaders and scholars to work on a prayer that schools can adopt if desired.

**7. Use the "bully pulpit" of the Oval Office to encourage church attendance.** President Trump often mentions faith in his speeches and public pronouncements. He can sharpen that message by encouraging attendance at church services—not just by his own example, but also by reminding people to seek out churches in their own communities. The point will be to reinforce church attendance as a norm in American life and to bring faith back to the center.

## Support a Culture of Life

Abortion has been one of the most contentious issues in the past half-century. In the past several years, anticipating the overturning of *Roe v. Wade*, Democrats have passed radical laws allowing abortion until birth. Conservatives have pushed for more restrictions. Two-thirds of Americans want to ban late-term abortions; two-thirds want to keep early abortion legal. In a post-*Dobbs* world, we will let the states decide. But we can also encourage a culture of life.

**1. Suspend and review all ongoing investigations of pro-life activists pursued by the Biden DOJ.** The Biden Department of Justice has pursued draconian sentences for peaceful protesters who dared to pray in abortion clinics or who have been confronted by violent pro-choice protesters. Meanwhile, the DOJ has ignored attacks on pregnancy centers. All ongoing investigations of pro-life activists must be suspended and reviewed for bias and prosecutorial abuse.

**2. Announce a DOJ task force to protect pregnancy centers.** "Pro-choice" should mean respecting all choices, including the choice to have a baby or to choose adoption. Yet pro-life pregnancy centers have been under attack from pro-abortion terrorists. The Department of Justice has made excuses, saying the attacks occur at night and are harder to patrol. The new administration will set up a task force to protect pregnancy centers and recommend new laws.

**3. Immediately cancel military subsidization of travel for abortion.** The Biden Department of Defense has spent federal dollars in the service of abortion, arguing it is necessary to retain female service members, and that abortion is a right. This is a devious way of avoiding the Hyde amendment, which bans federal spending on abortion. The new Trump administration will issue an executive order immediately banning the Department of Defense from subsidizing abortion.

**4. Create a blacklist of foreign organizations that promote or provide abortions.** The "Mexico City" policy prevents US taxpayer dollars from funding foreign organizations that promote abortion. First adopted by

President Ronald Reagan, the "Mexico City" policy is routinely canceled by Democratic administrations and reinstated by Republican ones. The policy can be strengthened by creating a blacklist of foreign organizations that provide abortions abroad, not just by cutting off their funding. The White House will publish the list of those organizations that have been barred from receiving funding under the "Mexico City" policy, making it more difficult for subsequent administrations to restore their funding in future.

**5. Create a White House task force to promote childbearing.** The US has seen a steep drop in the birth rate over the past two decades, bringing it into line with most other western industrialized societies—with the exception of Israel, which has seen the birthrate rise even among secular people. We need to study strategies for promoting childbearing, including financial incentives and cultural changes. Above all, we must promote childbearing as a priority.

**6. Promote pregnancy centers and adoption through presidential initiatives.** The White House should support efforts to promote childbirth and should lend moral support to organizations that provide financial support to new mothers. Just as the White House has promoted faith-based charities in the past, the White House should promote faith-based pregnancy centers that work to make the choice of keeping a baby an easier one to make.

**7. Protect IVF treatment and research and set up an ethical panel to discuss it.** For millions of parents, in vitro fertilization is the only path to parenthood. As a nation, we want to encourage parenthood and a culture of life. Recognizing that there are difficult ethical questions surrounding IVF, the Trump White House will set up a new ethical panel of experts to explore all of the difficult religious, scientific, and moral questions around IVF and make recommendations.

## Protect Religious Liberty

Religious liberty has been under assault in recent years. Secularists—sometimes in a well-intentioned but misguided effort to encourage tolerance—have driven religion out of the public realm. Worse, during the coronavirus pandemic, Democrats sought to ban religious worship for the sake of "social distancing" restrictions that, themselves, turned out not to be scientific. We need to restore due respect for religious liberty in our government and our culture.

**1. Appoint a commission to review actions taken against religious liberty during the pandemic.** There has never been accountability for the violations of religious liberty during the coronavirus pandemic, when governors in "blue" states shut down religious worship. The president should appoint a panel to develop a historical record of what happened and to make firm recommendations on the protection of religious liberty so that it never happens again.

**2. Establish August 21 as "Religious Liberty Day," commemorating Washington's letter to the Jews of Newport.** In his letter of August 21, 1790, President George Washington promised Jews that they would never have to live in fear in America, as they had in other lands. He also laid out the moral and philosophical foundations for religious liberty in the United States. August 21 should be an occasion for commemorating Washington's commitment to faith and freedom.

**3. Re-issue an executive order instructing the Treasury to restrict the application of the Johnson Amendment.** The Johnson Amendment prohibits religious groups and charities that are recognized as such by the Internal Revenue Service from engaging in political activity or endorsing political candidates. President Trump issued an executive order relaxing the use of this rule. He should reiterate that congregations will not be punished for their political speech.

**4. Establish religious exemptions for vaccines, abortion, and transgender surgery.** During the coronavirus pandemic, regulators often failed to recognize religious objections to vaccines. Moreover, there are many doctors who object to performing abortions or transgender surgery. The Trump administration can issue regulations to defend religious liberty and grant exemptions from these and other controversial practices that health care employees may encounter.

**5. Direct the DOJ to investigate civil rights violations by anti-Israel groups.** Jews have been the targets of aggressive campaigns of harassment—and worse—by anti-Israel groups on university campuses and in many cities. Under Biden, the DOJ's Civil Rights Division did nothing to investigate the organizations involved and their sources of funding. President Trump should direct the DOJ Civil Rights division to open an immediate and sweeping investigation.

**6. Establish a special envoy devoted to monitoring the persecution of Christians.** The White House has an antisemitism envoy whose job it is to monitor and counteract anti-Jewish prejudice, which is an urgent task. The persecution of Christians and the suppression of their religious liberty is likewise urgent and needs a devoted executive officer. President Trump will establish a special

envoy to fight anti-Christian prejudice, with ambassado-
rial rank.

**7. Link trade to religious liberty.** During the Cold War,
the US passed the Jackson-Vannik amendment, which
linked trade benefits for the Soviet Union to compliance
with human rights treaties. Similarly, the US should
link trade benefits to compliance with religious liberty. Countries that persecute Christians and members
of other faiths, like China and Iran, should not receive
favorable treatment in trade with the United States and
should face additional sanctions.

## Empower Faith Leaders

Faith is crucial to the improvement of American communities. The power of faith communities to change lives
was recognized over two decades ago with the creation
of the White House office of faith-based initiatives. But
the focus on religious pathways to poverty alleviation,
addiction recovery, and education has slipped recently,
as the focus has shifted to large government programs
and welfare spending. The White House will restore the
role of faith in public policy.

**1. Direct the Department of Education to study school
vouchers for parochial schools.** Experiments in several
states have shown that school vouchers can be used to

allow students to attend religious schools if the vouchers do not directly subsidize religious education. The Department of Education should prepare a study on the feasibility of legalizing such vouchers nationwide to subsidize religious education and increase access for disadvantaged children.

**2. Enlist faith-based organizations in the fight against the fentanyl pandemic.** Many 12-step programs include an element of faith, because belief in a higher power is often essential for those struggling to pull themselves out of the depths of addiction. President Trump should direct the Department of Health and Human Services and other agencies to provide grant funding for faith-based organizations to address the fentanyl crisis and the opioid pandemic generally.

**3. Provide grants for basic religious literacy education in public schools.** Students today know almost nothing about the basic religious texts of Judeo-Christian civilization. While local school districts retain control of curriculum decisions, the federal government should reallocate existing funds to the study of the Bible in a literary and historical context. Other religious texts can also be eligible for the funding, which will comply with the First Amendment.

**4. Ensure that faith-based organizations enjoy exemptions in programs that would require them to violate religious conscience.** For years, the Obama administration fought a legal battle against the Little Sisters of the Poor, a non-profit Catholic organization founded in the nineteenth century and run by nuns who provide services for the indigent elderly. Obama wanted to force the nuns to provide contraception in their health insurance plan for employees, against Catholic teachings. President Trump should issue an executive order exempting religious organizations from such onerous provisions.

**5. Highlight the role of faith in sports.** Christians should not have to go to the Supreme Court to fight for their right to pray on the football field or in locker rooms. The president should direct the Department of Education to make clear that it welcomes prayer during student athletic events at every level, as long as such prayers are not coercive or disruptive. Professional sports teams should also be encouraged to allow coaches and players to express faith on the field.

**6. Organize ecumenical meetings among faith leaders for common social goals.** Events like the National Prayer Breakfast happen once a year. But the need for shared religious leadership is constant. The White House should organize prayer meetings and scholarly exchanges among faith leaders to discuss a variety of topics of common concern, especially the fight against poverty, homelessness, drug addiction, and the struggle for family values.

**7. Create a new presidential medal for leadership within religious communities.** Just as the Medal of Freedom honors outstanding achievement in civilian life, the Presidential Medal of Faith could honor the contributions of clergy and lay leaders to the nation. An annual ceremony at the White House would recognize outstanding feats of religious scholarship; exceptional work in the fields of charity and service; and great accomplishments in the field of religious education.

# Chapter 5

# Identity Politics

## Embrace Equality and Reject 'Equity'

"Identity politics," broadly speaking, has had a devastating effect on American culture and society, destroying the unity of the American people and undermining our self-confidence. It divides human beings into groups according to race, gender, and other criteria, and sets us against each other in a competition for public resources and power. The new administration will take on identity politics, beginning with a focus on racial equality, not on racial division.

**1. Embrace equality and reject "equity."** The Biden administration made "equity"—which uses racial criteria to create an artificial equality of outcomes—the focus of government. In effect, that made racism once again the official policy of the United States, because it forces the government to treat people of different races differently. In doing so, ironically, "equity" reinforces racial stereotypes. "Equity" may also hurt those it intends to help by lowering the quality of government services upon which the poor depend. The Trump White House will repeal all of the executive orders and actions aimed at "equity," and restore classic "equality before the law" as the basic principle through which individuals are regarded by their government.

**2. Remove "Diversity, Equity, and Inclusion" from federal hiring and promotion.** DEI has become a tool for discrimination in the workplace and has caused large organizations, public and private, to become less productive and more obsessed with racial ideology. The Trump administration will remove DEI and restore compliance with the Civil Rights Act and other policies that seek out qualified candidates from disadvantaged backgrounds on a fair basis.

**3. Remove "Critical Race Theory" training from all government departments.** CRT is a radical idea that claims all American institutions are "systemically racist" because the country was founded when slavery was legal, thereby enshrining white supremacy. It is a radical ideology that has no place in government departments. The Trump administration will remove it from the government, including from racial sensitivity training manuals and diversity programs.

**4. Direct the Department of Education to remove "Critical Race Theory" from curricula.** Advocates of CRT have sought to introduce it into schools to indoctrinate children to regard their country with suspicion and to see themselves as members of racial groups first, and Americans second. President Trump will direct the Department of Education to remove CRT from curricula and to regard its presence negatively when evaluating the performance of educational institutions.

**5. Elevate neglected black role models from American history.** Today's political culture favors radicals over patriots—Malcolm X over Martin Luther King, Jr.— and victims over achievers—George Floyd over Booker T. Washington. The Trump administration will elevate great black American role models who are often neglected—starting with federal recognition of Booker T. Washington's birthday, April 5, as a day to focus on promoting vocational training.

**6. Establish the $200 bill featuring Harriet Tubman.** Several years ago, there was discussion of an effort to place Harriet Tubman, heroine of the Underground Railroad, on the $20 bill. But there is no need to displace American heroes like Andrew Jackson, who currently graces the bill. Instead, the Treasury department will be directed to issue a new $200 bill, which will feature Tubman's portrait, including her in the pantheon of American heroes honored on our currency.

**7. Focus student loan relief on Historically Black Colleges and Universities (HBCUs).** HBCUs lack resources other institutions may have that help to support graduates who do not earn enough money after graduation to service their student loans. Moreover, black graduates currently have default rates three times as high as white students. The Trump administration will launch a fund through which HBCUs can more easily raise money to support student loan relief.

## Restrain Transgenderism

The transgender phenomenon is disrupting the lives of many Americans. Transgenderism is based on gender dysphoria, a real condition that affects a tiny minority of people, mostly men. But lately, through social media and political activism, it has spread. The movement wants more than tolerance and non-discrimination: it wants to overturn the notion of gender itself. The new administration will protect communities, families, and children from radical transgenderism.

**1. Ban "gender-affirming" treatments, including drugs and surgery, for all minors.** There is no reason to allow, or to encourage, children to undergo irreversible medical interventions that will change their bodies forever, rendering some infertile and some unable to enjoy healthy sex lives. Children cannot possibly give informed consent to such interventions. President Trump will direct the Food and Drug Administration to protect children from transgender surgery and drugs.

**2. Direct all federal agencies to recognize only two genders.** Whatever people wish to identify with cannot change biology and cannot be imposed on others. Documentation from states that allow individuals to specify some other category of gender should not be recognized at the federal level. The federal government should take the position that there are two genders, corresponding to the two biological sexes, except in rare cases of chromosomal abnormality.

**3. Protect women's sports from transgender athletes.** The Department of Education must reverse its policies imposing transgenderism on women's sports, which allows biological males to compete with—and usually to dominate—female athletes. The president should indicate that the administration's policy is to regard transgenderism in sports as a violation of women's basic rights to equality under Title IX of the Civil Rights Act, and therefore to bar it accordingly.

**4. End transgenderism in the military except on a case-by-case basis.** Gender dysphoria is one of the only medical conditions that is not a disqualification from military service; those who join the military to take advantage of "gender-affirming" treatment may also be unable to work or to be deployed. The military can consider applications from transgender volunteers on a case-by-case basis but should otherwise return to the policy that existed before President Biden.

**5. Return to the policy of allowing states and school districts to decide.** In his first term, President Trump issued an executive order allowing states to make their own decisions on issues like transgender bathrooms, while President Biden has since adopted a policy that prevents states from issuing blanket bans on such bathrooms. President Trump will restore the previous policy while making it clear that the federal government opposes transgender bathrooms in K-12 schools.

**6. Adopt a policy that protects Americans from being forced to use non-biological pronouns.** Workplaces have been deferring to transgender ideology by punishing those who decline to use the pronouns chosen by individuals who decide that they want to identify themselves with non-biological gender labels, or substitute plural for singular pronouns. The Trump administration should protect those who simply want to use traditional pronouns.

**7. End federal government observances of transgender calendar events.** There is a proliferation of transgender awareness events on the calendar, many of which have been observed by the Biden administration. It is inappropriate for the federal government to adopt transgender ideology in any official capacity, beyond observing Supreme Court rulings on non-discrimination. Transgender individuals can be recognized within the LGBT whole, instead.

## Promote Diversity

Our national motto is *E pluribus unum*—"From many, one." Diversity is at the heart of what America is about. But we have reduced our definition of "diversity" to race, gender, and other crude categories, rather than honoring the diversity of our cultures and ideas. A misconception about diversity has led, ironically, to a "cancel culture" that silences dissident voices. We need to cultivate diversity of ideas and reject the conformity that is descending on American life.

**1. Direct the Department of Education to report on the state of intellectual diversity on campus.** There are anecdotal stories about the lack of conservative faculty and ideas on American campuses. It is important to know the depths of this problem, so that universities and the federal government can begin to address it. The president will order a study on political and intellectual diversity at these institutions, which are heavily funded by the federal taxpayers.

**2. Monitor compliance with Supreme Court decisions against the use of race in admissions.** Though Harvard lost at the Supreme Court in its effort to defend the use of racial criteria in admissions, Harvard and other elite universities have a pattern of working around such rulings by using other criteria that are substitutes for race. The Trump administration will monitor compliance with the Court's ruling to ensure that merit, not race, remains the focus.

**3. Develop a new journalism prize that is an alternative to the Polks and Pulitzers.** The American media is beset by ideological conformity that constrains democratic debate. The standard American journalism prizes—especially the Pulitzer—reinforce this sense of conformity by rewarding work that advances a left-wing narrative, regardless of the facts. The White House will develop its own journalism prize to reward the unbiased pursuit of truth.

**4. Direct the Federal Trade Commission to investigate social media companies for censorship.** The Silicon Valley tech giants have an inordinate amount of power over public discourse. They often censor critical voices and factual information that contradicts the politically correct narrative being pushed by those in power. The FTC should investigate social media censorship and expose the collusion between government and Silicon Valley to suppress ideas.

**5. Prohibit the Securities and Exchange Commission (SEC) from demanding DEI information from companies.** Criteria such as ESG (environmental, social, and governance) and DEI are metrics that are used to enforce conformity with left-wing ideology on Wall Street. The result is that companies become less profitable when they are less interested in an employee's promise and skill, or in investments that might grow the economy to create more opportunity for all.

**6. Redirect National Public Radio Funds to Community Stations.** It is unconscionable that a "national" radio news network, which obtains part of its funding (however small) from the federal government, should be so left-wing and so biased in favor of the Democratic Party. NPR will survive a withdrawal of federal funding, but it will be less able to keep competitors from emerging. Funding to local community radio stations can continue—provided that the funds are not used to subsidize NPR itself.

**7. End Net Neutrality, which is making a comeback at the FCC.** Net Neutrality sells itself as a way to ensure access to the Internet. In practice, it risks restricting investment in broadband technologies, therefore reducing access to the Internet. The Internet needs to be kept as free as possible, not subjected to further government regulation—especially after the government has shown it is capable of censoring debate online. Only a free approach ensures diversity of views.

## Embrace Patriotism

Instead of identity politics, we need to strengthen our common identity as Americans—an identity that transcends race, gender, religion, sexuality, and all other categories. The reason America has succeeded is that successive waves of immigrants have sought to assimilate and have contributed to our collective national culture in the process. We need to reinforce the shared values and ideals that make us Americans, building a culture of patriotism and tolerance.

**1. Ban the display of flags other than the American flag at US embassies and government buildings.** Except for state visits and the like, where leaders from other countries are present, no flag should fly along with the US flag on our embassies. In recent years, Democratic administrations have flown various versions of the LGBTQ "rainbow pride" flag, as well as the Black Lives Matter flag. These are partisan flags and do not represent the country.

**2. Reinforce the idea that there is only one national anthem.** Recently, the NFL began playing two anthems— the *Star-Spangled Banner* and *Lift Every Voice and Sing*. While the latter is a part of America's cultural heritage, it is not our national anthem, and its use creates the mistaken impression that we are a nation defined by racial divisions. The president will take executive action to promote the *Star-Spangled Banner* as the single anthem of our country.

**3. Reestablish the Fourth of July military parade.** In 2019, President Donald Trump hosted the "Salute to America," a national celebration of American independence that featured flyovers from different branches of the US military. The idea was to make the celebration a national tradition. The pandemic disrupted those plans, and there has not been a similar celebration since. President Trump would take executive action to establish an annual "Salute to America."

**4. Direct the creation of a national memorial to the victims of communism.** America won the Cold War—but forgot why we fought it. Two generations of young Americans have come of age without learning that communism was, and still is, evil. If anything, young Americans are being taught to embrace communist ideals. We need a museum and memorial to honor the millions of victims of communism, and to pay homage to those who fought it throughout the twentieth century.

**5. Develop the National Garden of American Heroes.** President Trump proposed the creation of a national sculpture garden to honor American heroes from a diversity of backgrounds and walks of life. However, President Biden rescinded that proposal. The next Trump administration should revive it and direct federal agencies to work together to identify a suitable site, one in which America's inspiring natural beauty and national heritage can complement one another.

**6. Develop a national bicycle trail.** Though there are extensive bicycle trails in many major cities, and through some state and federal parks, the US lacks a national bicycle trail. The trail would reinforce a sense of unity and allow cyclists to cross the entire continental United States. Modeled after the Appalachian Trail, it would draw Americans and visitors to experience the beauty of our country. President Trump would direct a planning effort to identify possible routes.

**7. Hold a parade to honor veterans of the war against terror.** After 9/11, millions of Americans stepped up to defend the country. They fought in Afghanistan, Iraq, and around the world to secure our nation, destroying Al Qaeda and ISIS. We have never properly honored the veterans of that struggle with an appropriate parade and commemoration. President Trump will hold a celebration of the veterans of the war against terror, restoring a post-9/11 sense of unity.

## Chapter 6

# Economy

## Lower Inflation

The most serious economic challenge we face today is inflation. When President Trump left office in 2021, inflation was below 2 percent. Within just a few months of President Biden taking office, it had skyrocketed to nearly 10 percent after Biden and the Democrats passed massive spending bills. The Federal Reserve has raised interest rates, but the American dream remains out of touch for many Americans. There are several steps a new president can take to fight inflation.

**1. Slash government departments.** Argentinian president Javier Milei bought down his government's soaring inflation by eliminating government departments and firing tens of thousands of government workers. The

US president lacks the power to shut down departments completely, but can eliminate positions within those departments. President Trump will undertake a massive cut in federal government jobs that will reduce federal spending.

**2. Move government departments out of Washington, DC.** There is no reason that every government department has to be in Washington, one of the most expensive cities in the US. The federal government should be dispersed throughout the fifty US states, providing an economic boom to local communities and reducing costs and congestion in the nation's capital, as well as reducing the political power of Washington within the American federal system.

**3. Stop expanding student loan bailouts.** The Biden administration tried forgiving student loans and was blocked by the Supreme Court. But it found loopholes that allowed it to continue. Doing so meant that certain groups of people were suddenly able to spend more money—adding to inflationary pressures. The new administration will halt the student loan bailouts that Biden has used to buy support, which have only worsened the inflation problem he created.

**4. Declare an intention to veto budgets that are not moving toward balance.** The congressional spending spree must stop. Although the spending power belongs to Congress and not to the president, the president can veto spending bills. President Trump should compel Congress to move toward balanced budgets by using his veto pen to reject congressional spending that does not put the US on track to return to the balanced budgets of the 1990s.

**5. Remove restrictions on domestic energy production.** The new administration will adopt a completely new policy on energy (see Chapter 7). By expanding domestic energy production, the second Trump administration can change expectations about future oil and gas prices and increase domestic supplies. That, in turn, can have the effect of lowering fuel prices, which are a major driver of inflationary pressures, since fuel costs affect every link in the supply chain.

**6. Replace Federal Reserve chairman Jerome Powell.** The Fed chair raised interest rates too quickly throughout 2019, slowing economic growth. Then he lowered them too dramatically in 2020, helping to lay the foundations for the inflationary spiral that followed. Now the Fed has raised interest rates, putting home ownership out of reach for many. The Fed has also been distracted by political issues beyond monetary policy. New leadership is needed in 2026.

**7. Revisit unspent coronavirus relief funds.** There are billions of dollars that were allocated for coronavirus relief that have yet to be spent. Though the president is restricted by the Impoundment Control Act and cannot stop money from being spent, he can direct the Office of Management and Budget to itemize the spending that has not yet taken place in various departments and ask Congress to claw back the funds though cuts to subsequent budgets.

## Boost Growth

The foundation of any successful economic policy must be growth. Democrats often focus on redistribution—taxing some to subsidize others—and leave growth as an afterthought. At one point, President Biden presided over two consecutive quarters of negative growth. Economic growth recovered, but it is slowing down today because the administration remains stuck in old and failed big-government ideas. President Trump will make economic growth his top priority.

**1. Protect American industry and manufacturing.** Foreign competitors, notably China, are continuing to take advantage of American markets while also stealing cutting-edge American technology. Just as the US imposed tariffs on China in the first Trump administration, the US will aggressively target Chinese goods and

Chinese manufacturers, including in the electric vehicle (EV) market, so that US manufacturers can compete on a level playing field.

**2. Restore the two-for-one rule to cut regulations that stifle innovation and investment.** Under President Trump, the federal government could not make one new regulation unless it would also destroy two. President Biden has returned the bureaucrats to power, and regulations are proliferating again. President Trump should restore the two-for-one rule to ensure that the reach of the federal government is once again held in check and the private sector can flourish.

**3. Unleash energy projects and innovation.** The next administration should free up oil-rich federal land again for exploration and development (see Chapter 7). It should also expand nuclear power, alongside all of the investment and rhetoric that is promoting renewables. President Trump should issue an executive order stating clearly that economic growth and job creation will be the top priorities in energy policy, and environmental groups will not have a veto.

**4. Introduce E-Verify to ensure Americans have priority in jobs.** The influx of illegal migrants has boosted overall jobs numbers but has led to a higher unemployment rate for Americans and has increased downward pressure on wages. Wages rose, particularly for minorities, when the Trump administration cracked down on illegal immigration. President Trump will direct the federal government to develop an E-Verify system that can confirm workers' immigration status.

**5. Declare the any new income tax increases will be vetoed.** President Biden wants to raise taxes on those he describes as wealthy—adding that they need to pay their "fair share." He himself has evaded taxes, and high earners typically pay disproportionately higher taxes. Rather than letting the Tax Cuts and Jobs Act provisions expire, Congress should renew them—and the president should be ready with his veto pen to reject any new tax increases from Capitol Hill.

**6. Embrace the AI revolution and move chip manufacturing to the US.** China is determined to monopolize the global production of chips needed for AI technology—by invading Taiwan, if necessary. President Trump will issue executive orders establishing the goal of making the US the number one AI chip maker in the world, declaring the supply of chips as a key strategic asset, and using emergency powers to help chip manufacturers bypass regulations and taxes.

**7. Build the infrastructure that Biden promised but failed to deliver.** President Biden signed a $2 trillion infrastructure bill into law—thanks to Republicans, who said at the time President Trump took office that $1 trillion was too much to spend on infrastructure. But more than two years later, very little has been built. By mid-2024, only about eight of the 500,000 EV charging stations had been built. Trump will set aside red tape to get the EV infrastructure built.

## Improve Health and Education

Health care and education are the foundation of a productive workforce. But health insurance costs remain high; life expectancy is falling, and productivity is in decline. Biden's sole health care achievement is to re-do a Trump policy—lowering the cost of insulin, which he revoked upon taking office, only to claim credit for reductions later. And education continues to struggle thanks to Biden's left-wing allies. Donald Trump will be the health and education president.

**1. Issue waivers to allow cheaper, short-term health insurance policies.** Obamacare policies remain too expensive for many Americans who are not eligible for, or do not want, Medicaid at the state level. President Trump will direct the Department of Health and Human Services (HHS) to issue waivers for insurance policies that are cheap, offer basic coverage, and enable younger workers or those switching careers to bridge the gap without fear.

**2. Expand telehealth options to lower costs and increase access.** President Trump enabled the growth of telehealth services during the coronavirus pandemic, when Americans could not easily visit doctors. The Biden administration rolled back those services by expanding regulations. President Trump would use executive orders to waive regulations on telehealth services and allow Americans to enjoy cheaper and more efficient everyday consultations.

**3. Establish a voluntary health ID with debit access for health savings accounts.** Health care providers often require an insurance card to be presented, along with a trove of other information. The Trump administration will direct HHS to offer voluntary ID cards that can store information about an individual's health insurance coverage and medical records, and that can be linked to Health Savings Accounts through a debit system compatible with banking hardware.

**4. Direct HHS to allow insurance companies to reward positive fitness behaviors.** Health insurance companies focus on risks but largely ignore rewards—such as joining a gym, quitting smoking, or committing to a nutritional plan. President Trump should direct HHS to explore regulatory allowances for health insurance companies to offer premium discounts to those Americans who engage in healthier behaviors as a form of preventative medicine.

**5. Use federal student loans to support vocational training programs, not just college.** With the value of a college degree decreasing, and the value of specific skills and certifications increasing, many Americans are considering vocational training as an alternative to academic training. The Trump administration will direct federal student loan programs to develop loans for American adults of all ages who wish to obtain vocational skills at accredited institutions.

**6. Redesign federal student loan programs so that universities are on the hook.** One of the main drivers of the rise in higher education costs, ironically, is the support of the federal government, which allows universities to raise tuition and pass on the costs. The Trump administration will require higher education institutions to act as guarantors for student loans, making them focus on giving students skills that can actually help them repay their loans.

**7. Pledge to veto any educational appropriations that do not include funding for DC voucher programs.** Democrats have tried to cancel a successful school voucher program in the District of Columbia, as they have attacked similar programs elsewhere. President Trump should issue s preemptive declaration that he will veto any bill that fails to provide the needed appropriations to continue the DC Opportunity Scholarships program for needy students.

## Encourage Families

The cost of running a family—especially the cost of childcare—has emerged as a major economic challenge for American families. Beyond the burden of inflation generally, the cost of childcare discourages parents, particularly mothers, from seeking job opportunities. It also discourages parents from having additional children, which in turn contributes to the declining birthrate. President Trump will encourage families by easing the cost of raising children.

**1. Establish a panel of experts to study the costs and benefits of paid maternity leave.** During the first Trump administration, presidential adviser (and daughter) Ivanka Trump suggested the US join other countries in offering paid maternity leave. Though a program of that size will require congressional authorization and spending, it could pay for itself by increasing income and income tax revenues. President Trump will convene experts to study the proposal.

**2. Establish a White House office devoted to lowering family costs.** Because of the role of families in raising children, and because the collapsing birthrate is becoming a national emergency, it is necessary to appoint an expert within the White House to work on ideas and proposals to lower the costs of starting families and raising children. The proposals could be shaped into legislation that the president would urge Congress to support for his signature.

**3. Encourage states to develop ways of paying for maternity leave other than the state unemployment bureaucracy.** In many states, maternity leave is paid for through the state unemployment system. In many states, that system is slow, meaning mothers who need an income while they are caring for children in the first weeks of their lives cannot access the funds in time. The president will direct the Department of Labor to recommend alternative approaches.

**4. Explore insurance subsidies for parents seeking in vitro fertilization (IVF).** In addition to the panel of experts that the president will convene to study and resolve the emerging ethical questions about IVF, the president should direct HHS to develop ways in which insurance companies can begin to offer coverage for fertility treatments, which are typically paid out of pocket.

Bringing down the cost of IVF for families will help make childbearing more affordable.

**5. Encourage multigenerational families by expanding the definition of "dependents" for tax purposes.** President Trump can direct the Treasury and the Internal Revenue Service to expand the definition of "dependents" to allow grandparents to include grandchildren to whom they provide regular care. This can provide an incentive for multigenerational families to share in the tasks of raising children—and to be rewarded when they do so, lowering child care costs.

**6. Direct the Office of Management and Budget to count household labor in a measure of Gross Domestic Product.** The work that parents, especially mothers, perform at home is usually informal and therefore not measured in statistics such as the Gross Domestic Product. But there are ways such work can be valued and measured, which implies there can also be ways to subsidize it. President Trump will direct OMB to develop a new "household" indicator.

**7. Use the "bully pulpit" to highlight the positive contributions of mothers.** The Trump White House can enhance the prestige of parenthood in general and motherhood in particular by featuring the contributions of American mothers in White House events and communications.

Mother's Day—a commercial holiday—is not enough; the White House should make motherhood a focus and encourage Americans to see it as a goal, rather than a burden.

# Chapter 7

# Energy

## Reverse Bans

The Biden administration picked up where the Obama administration left off in its assault on US energy production. Though oil production hit record highs, that was—like the shale oil boom under Obama—in spite of administration policy, not because of it. Biden's policies have led to rising gas prices, industry layoffs, and a weakening of the US economy. President Trump will restore the US energy sector—beginning with the reversal of several Biden policies.

**1. Lift the ban on new liquefied natural gas (LNG) exports.** The Biden administration has paused new approvals of LNG exports, supposedly for the "public interest" of fighting climate change. Ironically, that pause has increased European dependence on Russia as a source of fossil fuels, just as the US is trying to maintain Europe's support for Ukraine against Russian invasion. President Trump will lift the ban and allow US LNG to continue to supply the world.

**2. Lift restrictions on the production and transport of natural gas.** The reason the US has been able to grow its economy while reducing its emissions over the last several years has been the boom in natural gas as an energy source. However, the Biden administration has sought to restrict the growth of that sector with a variety of unnecessary regulations. The Trump administration will review and cancel most of those regulations to allow natural gas to flourish.

**3. Reverse the Biden restrictions on offshore oil and gas leases.** The Biden administration has tried to block offshore oil and gas development even where it can be done safely and where existing industry infrastructure means the environmental cost is low. The restrictions on offshore development are meant to fight climate change, but they would have minimal impact on global surface temperatures. The Trump administration will reopen responsible offshore energy leases.

**4. Reopen the Arctic National Wildlife Refuge (ANWR) to oil and gas leasing.** The Biden administration canceled leases issued during the Trump administration, after Congress voted to open up the Arctic coastal plain to oil and gas development. The area can be safely developed, but that has not stopped Biden from putting it off-limits—along with the National Petroleum Reserve-Alaska (NPR-A), which President Trump will also reopen to oil and gas leasing.

**5. Cancel Biden policies on carbon-free energy sector by 2035 and "net zero" by 2050.** The US economy cannot be responsibly run on renewable energy alone—certainly not in the absence of large-scale nuclear power. Fossil fuels remain crucial to our energy mix. That is why President Trump will cancel the unnecessary and distortionary goals of the Biden administration to achieve a "carbon pollution-free power sector" by 2035 and "net zero" emissions by 2050.

**6. Cancel coal power rules that are aimed at killing the industry.** The Biden administration, again picking up where the Obama administration left off, developed a set of rules for coal plants that aims to phase out coal entirely as an energy source, despite its abundance. (Biden promised in West Virginia in 2008 that he and Obama would commit to "clean coal.") The new administration should cancel these rules and allow coal to continue within the US energy mix.

*The Agenda*

**7. Approve the Keystone XL pipeline.** The Obama administration blocked the Keystone XL pipeline, in deference to environmental activists, even though it had passed every approval process. The Trump administration immediately approved the project, but President Biden canceled it as soon as he took office, killing thousands of jobs—including union jobs. Though largely symbolic at this stage, an approval would send a positive signal about US energy.

## Expand Options

Environmentalists aim to push the US toward a "net zero" future that is entirely dependent on renewables like solar and wind. But those sources are not robust during bouts of unfavorable weather and cannot reasonably produce enough power for America's needs. Whether we believe in "climate change" or not, what we need is an "all-of-the-above" approach that uses different sources and guarantees energy security. President Trump will develop a diverse array of energy sources.

**1. Accelerate development of nuclear power.** Even Biden realizes that nuclear power is necessary for producing energy without increasing carbon emissions. But the administration has not prioritized nuclear energy, has not eased regulations, and has not asked Congress for resources to develop nuclear resources. The new administration will accelerate nuclear power by cutting unnecessary regulations and reallocating Department of Energy funds to nuclear.

**2. Encourage new hydroelectric power resources.** States like California started to move toward building new reservoirs for water storage but these have become bogged down in regulatory mazes and political disputes, with the federal government only providing minimal support. The Trump administration will waive regulations to accelerate water storage and hydroelectric power development and will allocate infrastructure funds for hydroelectric power.

**3. Change regulations to allow private households to make money from solar power.** In the early days of solar power, households looked forward to being able to make money by providing surplus power to the grid. But state regulations have hampered that process at the behest of utility monopolies. President Trump will direct the Federal Trade Commission and the Department of Justice to intervene, and to expand solar power by allowing households to profit.

**4. Accelerate research into new vertical turbines for wind power.** Conventional wind turbines are bulky, difficult to maintain, and dangerous for birds. Newer, vertical-axis wind turbines could produce more power over less area, making wind power more efficient and less disruptive. President Trump will direct the Department of Energy to fund research in vertical-axis wind turbines and to accelerate approval for power facilities that use the vertical-axis model.

**5. Ease approval for geothermal energy projects.** The US is slowly expanding research into geothermal energy, which involves drilling deep holes and injecting water into hot areas in the earth's crust, and using the resultant steam to drive turbines. The new administration will direct the Department of Energy to expand research funding grants and will ease the process of converting existing oil and gas leases into geothermal permits, which use similar technology.

**6. Invest in coal-to-oil technology.** An energy process that converts coal to synthetic oil has been known for decades, but is not used widely in the US. Given the vast coal resources of the United States—centuries' worth of coal in Alaska, for example—there is no reason the US should not be using existing technology to produce more oil and conducting additional research in the field. President Trump should direct the Department of Energy to prioritize coal-to-oil.

**7. Invest in new energy technologies that could add to the mix.** The US should prioritize research into new energy sources, such as fusion, and into improvements in existing alternative energy sources, such as biomass and other older technologies. To that end, the president can direct the Department of Energy to make more research funds available, and can award an annual Energy Prize for the most significant innovations in energy science and technology.

## Build Infrastructure

America's transportation network is failing. Biden and the Democrats spent trillions on so-called "infrastructure," with nothing to show for it. That is because only a small fraction of the spending went to roads and bridges, and because Biden does not know how to get things done. Secretary of Transportation Pete Buttigieg has a consultant's level of knowledge—which is to say, none at all. We need a builder to make infrastructure investments work, "green" and otherwise.

**1. Prioritize roads and bridges by implementing specific deadlines for states to act or lose funds.** The collapse of the Francis Scott Key bridge in Baltimore only highlighted our nation's dependence on old infrastructure. The Trump administration will tell states to prioritize the building of roads and bridges, while setting benchmarks and deadlines for achievement. Those state governments that delay should face the cancelation of federal funding, which will go to other states instead.

**2. End electric vehicle (EV) mandates and emissions standards that eliminate gas-powered cars.** The Biden administration has imposed electric vehicle mandates and emissions targets that are so strict they all but ensure that automakers will no longer be able to produce gas-powered cars. Yet consumers are rejecting electric vehicles. The Trump administration will cancel these mandates. Tesla has shown they are not necessary to drive consumer interest.

**3. Accelerate the buildup of electric vehicle (EV) charging stations.** Though EVs should not be mandated, the fact is that the market is growing, and the money is available to build the kind of national charging network that is necessary to make EVs attractive to drivers. But the Biden administration effort has been bogged down in bureaucracy. The Trump administration will cut through red tape by waiving environmental and other regulations for EV charging stations.

**4. Secure and upgrade America's electricity grid.** The US electricity grid remains vulnerable to security breaches that could knock out power for millions of people for extended periods of time, and that could cause major economic disruptions. In addition, growing demand in the face of decreasing supply—thanks to the rush to renewables—is straining the grid. The new administration will declare an emergency and direct infrastructure funds to secure the grid.

**5. Cancel high-speed rail grants to states for unprofitable projects.** Only a small number of the high-speed rail projects funded by the federal government have any chance of being profitable. The San Francisco-to-Los Angeles "bullet" train will not run and should be completely defunded; only a train from Los Angeles to Las Vegas is profitable, and even that should not depend on the government. The Trump administration will act quickly to recover the funds.

**6. Accelerate upgrades to America's airports.** Most US airports are still embarrassingly run-down and congested. With trillions of dollars in infrastructure spending, spending has been slow. The Trump administration will accelerate every step of the building and renovation process—from design, to permitting, to regulatory compliance. As with roads and bridges, funding that is not used quickly will be reallocated to other projects. An executive order will outline the plan.

**7. End DEI in Air Traffic Control and other related, essential fields.** The nation's air traffic is too important and too vulnerable to risk using DEI policies that value identity over skills. The Federal Aviation Administration (FAA) has spent too much time on DEI and "woke" ideology in the workplace, and not enough on making sure America's air fleet is safe to fly, and that planes in the air can navigate safely. The new administration will also bar DEI in other essential fields.

## Protect Our National Heritage

While developing America's energy sources, we must also protect our environment. These two priorities need not be contradictory; in many cases they are compatible. We have been misled into seeing them as opposites, because the Biden administration confuses "climate change"—a global phenomenon not primarily caused by pollutants—with protecting the environment from byproducts of industry. The new administration will protect America's natural heritage.

**1. Rename the Environmental Protection Agency as the Department of Conservation.** America's ethos needs to shift from the impractical utopianism of John Muir to the pragmatic conservationism of Gifford Pinchot. That is—our goal cannot be to lock the environment away in an imaginary pristine state, but rather to act as wise stewards of our natural resources. The new Trump administration will rename the department and redefine its mission accordingly.

**2. End poaching at sea.** For decades, fishing companies, mostly from Asia, have poached marine wildlife on the high seas, including endangered species. The Trump administration will deploy the US Navy and the Coast Guard to end poaching and will approach international forums to apply sanctions and other punishments to countries who allow private fleets to overharvest fisheries or to kill rare marine species that are at imminent risk of extinction.

**3. Round up plastics in the Pacific Ocean.** The Trump administration will help restore the health of our oceans by empowering the National Oceanic and Atmospheric Administration (NOAA), together with the US Navy, to invest in technologies that can learn up the "Great Pacific Garbage Patch." The cost will be recovered from nations that are determined to be the origin of the garbage, through actions pursued in US courts and in international tribunals.

**4. Empower the US Fish and Wildlife Service to remove invasive species.** For decades, zebra mussels in the ballast of international ships, as well as Asian carp swimming up our rivers, have interfered with our ecosystems, as have invasive plant and animal species on land. The US Fish and Wildlife Service will be given a new responsibility: to remove invasive species and to cite those who bring them to the United States, whether deliberately or through negligence.

**5. Invest in desalination and water-from-air technologies.** New technologies—many of which have been developed by our close ally, Israel—excel at turning seawater into potable water; turning wastewater into drinking water; and even drawing water from ambient air. The new water can recharge aquifers and rivers. Given the likelihood of water shortages in the future, the new administration will prioritize desalination and cut red tape to speed up permits.

**6. Prioritize farmers and hunters in resource allocation.** The environment should be managed for human benefit. That means farmers should receive larger allocations from federal water projects in states like California. It also means that hunters should receive permits on a generous basis to take species that are abundant and that may even be too dominant in some ecosystems. The primary users of these resources must be trusted to conserve them with care.

**7. Allow logging in national forests to remove old wood and create firebreaks.** One of the reasons for massive wildfires in the west in recent years is the exclusion of logging companies from lands once managed for their benefit. Old growth provides fuel for fires; logging roads can also create firebreaks that slow the spread of blazes. It is time to manage our forests properly rather than creating new hazards to the environment and to communities through neglect.

# Chapter 9

# The Debt

## Restructure the Debt

The US debt is skyrocketing. It is now nearly $35 trillion, and has skyrocketed in the past two decades, thanks to the war against terror, the coronavirus pandemic, and massive domestic spending. Democrats blame tax cuts for the debt, but there is no way to erase the debt by taxing our way out of it, and raising taxes would be self-defeating because it would slow economic growth. Creative ideas are needed, beginning with restructuring the debt to manage it.

**1. End debt limit increases.** The Trump administration will announce that the president will no longer sign congressional legislation to increase the debt limit. Past increases have only been an invitation to spend more without making the tough decisions that are necessary to control spending. If Congress chooses to override the president's veto and raise the debt limit anyway, it will bear that responsibility, but knowing a veto is waiting ought to spur Congress to act.

**2. Convene another debt commission.** After Congress passed the Budget Control Act in 2011, a bipartisan commission, led by former Republican Senator Alan Simpson and former Clinton White House chief of staff Erskine Bowles, met to recommend ways to fix temporary deficits and the long-term debt problem. The Obama administration refused to push its recommendations. The Trump administration will convene a new debt commission and back its policy proposals.

**3. Offer fifty-year and hundred-year Treasury bonds to restructure American debt.** The idea of offering long-term Treasury bonds was first considered in 2019 by Treasury Secretary Steven Mnuchin. It was never taken up, but the debt at that point was much smaller than it is today. The Trump administration will offer long-term Treasury bonds to allow the US to service its current debts at lower rates to enable repayment without major impact to current government needs.

**4. Study reforms of existing mandatory spending and entitlements.** Entitlements are taking up a huge portion of the budget. President Trump has promised not to touch Social Security and Medicare. For young new workers, however, a new approach is needed—one that works more like a personal savings account for Social Security, and personal health insurance for Medicare. The new administration will establish a bipartisan commission to study alternatives for reform.

**5. Keep corporate tax rates low and competitive.** The Tax Cuts and Jobs Act cut taxes for millions of middle-class Americans and slashed the top corporate tax rate from 35 percent (one of the highest in the world) to a competitive 21 percent (one of the lowest). Raising taxes would depress economic growth and lead to more tax evasion, meaning revenues would not rise. President Trump would promise to veto tax increases that are proposed as a way to pay down the debt.

**6. Start a national sovereign wealth fund that includes cryptocurrency.** President Trump will propose a "rainy day" fund within the Treasury, into which the US will deposit a mix of dollars, Bitcoin, and cryptocurrencies. The "rainy day" fund can act as a sovereign wealth investment fund whose assets, including such cryptocurrencies as Congress may issue to service the debt, can offset the nation's liabilities. Such a fund should have a politically independent board.

**7. Launch claims of resources in space that can be used as assets to offset debt.** As space exploration becomes more accessible, and as manned flights return to the moon and aim for Mars, the US can claim ownership of resources in space that can then be leased, sold, or leveraged to pay down existing national debt. The president will issue an executive order to establish sovereign ownership of assets in space, whether taken by private or public missions.

## Cut Spending and Costs

The size and scope of the federal government keep expanding. While the president does not have the power simply to shut down entire government departments, as President Javier Milei has done in Argentina, he can force job cuts, and as the country's chief executive officer, he can develop plans to reorganize the government while his appointees manage their own departments to achieve cost savings. Here are some cost-cutting steps Trump should take.

**1. Order most Cabinet secretaries to produce plans to cut spending within their departments to 2001 levels.** Much of the national debt has been accrued over the past two and a half decades. Cabinet secretaries should develop plans—with help from private consultants if necessary— to slash costs to 2001 levels, with the exception of the

Departments of Defense and Homeland Security, whose functions are essential and cannot be replicated.

**2. Announce that any proposed spending over the reduced levels will be vetoed.** Once targets have been set to cut spending, as above, the president should announce that spending bills that allocate funds to government departments, in excess of White House requests, will be vetoed—unless those spending bills also contain a provision that allows the government to direct any unspent funds toward paying down the national debt rather than other spending programs.

**3. Instruct the Department of Interior to develop plans to sell key mineral lands and assets to private industry.** The Department controls vast swathes of public land, including areas rich in oil and minerals. These, if sold, can help pay down the national debt. Regulations will need to be developed to ensure that buyers are majority-owned by US corporations and that land use will comply with laws on resource development and environmental protection.

**4. Develop plans to close or downsize certain government departments.** Several government departments are bigger and more expensive than they need to be. The Department of Education, for example, cannot be said to have improved education since it began in the

Carter administration. The functions of the Department of Housing and Urban Development can be performed by state and local governments. These are just two that can be targeted.

**5. Instruct the Department of Justice to investigate waste at every level of government.** The pandemic spending was necessary to save the US economy but was also subject to fraud on a massive scale. Fraud is ongoing in major programs. For example, some families hire their own relatives as "caregivers" and obtain reimbursement from Medicaid, which is run by the states, but also funded heavily by the federal government. Wasteful spending must be cut.

**6. Use unspent coronavirus funds to pay down the national debt.** As discussed earlier in the section on inflation, the White House can direct the Office of Management and Budget to identify unspent coronavirus relief funds and ask Congress to recover it. When it does so, the funding should be used to pay down the national debt rather than re-allocated to other purposes, just as with surplus tax revenues, so that debt elimination has priority in spending.

**7. Develop plans to spin off government bureaus as private companies that can raise capital in the markets.** In addition to developing plans for budget cuts, the president can direct that certain agencies whose functions are of interest to the private sector, like the Department of Energy, should consider privatizing portions of their operation. These could form state-owned private companies that can raise capital and whose capital assets can offset the national debt.

Chapter 10

# The Constitution

## Restore the Constitution

The past few years have seen an unprecedented assault on our Constitution by the left, which resents the checks and balances of our nation's founding document and the individual liberties of our Bill of Rights. If destroying the balance of powers or crushing due process rights helps Democrats to maintain control or to achieve what they define as a socially just outcome, they will do it. The next administration must take urgent steps to restore basic civics in the federal government.

**1. Require all executive department employees to pass the basic citizenship test.** Too many people working for the federal government do not have an elementary knowledge of the Constitution or the country's history.

All executive department employees—including political appointees—should have to pass the same citizenship test that we require immigrants to take. If they fail,
they should not be allowed to take posts in the federal
government until they pass.

**2. Call a conference aimed at organizing an Article
V convention.** Under Article V of the Constitution, a
conference can be organized to propose constitutional
amendments if two-thirds of the states agree. There are
several amendments—such as term limits for Congress—
that are necessary to restore the original spirit of our
Constitution (see Mark Levin's 2013 book, *The Liberty
Amendments*, which proposes eleven such changes).
Though two-thirds of states have not yet agreed, a White
House conference could help build momentum toward
the threshold.

**3. Rein in the power of Silicon Valley social media
companies.** The Silicon Valley giants can control what
Americans see and share online. In 2020, they censored
the Hunter Biden laptop story; in so doing, they interfered with the election. They also worked with the Biden
White House to suppress dissenting views on the coronavirus pandemic. The FTC will be directed to take
legal action against them to uphold free speech, or face
lawsuits that challenge their immunity.

**4. Launch civil rights investigations of universities that deny free speech.** In addition to civil rights investigations by the Department of Justice relating to the mistreatment of Jews on college campuses, the Department of Education Office of Civil Rights should investigate the suppression of conservative views by our nation's universities. Universities like Harvard that privilege some views and suppress others should face litigation and penalties for their abuses.

**5. Release a list of constitutional conservatives who will be considered for judicial appointments.** In 2016, then-candidate Trump won support from conservatives after he published a list of possible judicial appointments that had been vetted by the Federalist Society. In a second term, President Trump can publish a similar judicial list—and make clear his criteria for joining the list, namely a commitment to the originalist approach to the Constitution.

**6. Direct the department of Alcohol, Tobacco, Firearms and Explosives (AFT) to honor conceal carry licenses nationwide.** Universal recognition of conceal carry licenses—what proponents call "constitutional carry"— advances Second Amendment rights and ensures that Americans who qualify for those licenses in one state can defend themselves in another. It will also, contrary to left-wing propaganda, reduce crime, which is out of control in major cities.

**7. Repeal unconstitutional executive orders and actions by the Biden administration.** President Biden openly defied the Supreme Court on student loans, rent moratoria, and other topics, as he issued executive orders or took actions aimed at appeasing his base regardless of their constitutionality. The new administration will review all Biden administration actions and regulations for their constitutionality and repeal all that fail to honor the spirit of the Constitution.

## Protect Elections

Voting is the essence of constitutional democracy. Yet Americans no longer have faith in our elections, which have been distorted beyond recognition by new rules that depart from a previous norms and all notions of fairness. Though voting remains controlled by the states, there is much that the federal government can do to establish clear principles for free and fair elections, and to protect the processes through which voters make choices at the ballot box.

**1. Establish an independent, bipartisan commission for observing elections.** The Department of Justice only addresses serious cases of election fraud; neither it nor any other agency offers general observations of the electoral process. The new Trump administration will establish an Independent Electoral Commission to observe state and local election processes and grade them according to a list of objective criteria, flagging problems as they occur.

**2. Adopt the international norms of free and fair elections.** The Inter-Parliamentary Union has established criteria for free and fair elections. Though Americans tend to avoid using international resources to judge our own laws and political systems, in this case the rules are inspired by America's own past practices. The president can direct the Independent Electoral Commission to use these criteria when measuring whether elections have been free and fair.

**3. Direct the federal government to observe Election Day as a public holiday.** Rather than using extended periods of early voting, or vote-by mail, the best way to expand ballot access is to make Election Day a public holiday. Though it takes an act of Congress to establish an official public holiday, the president can use his authority as the chief executive officer of the US to close federal public offices on Election Day, except essential services and voting-related offices.

**4. Direct the Election Assistance Commission (EAC) to subtract federal grant money from any states using private funding.** In 2020, private donors, such as Mark Zuckerberg, spent as much as the federal government on election operations. This money was spent almost exclusively to help Democrats turn out the vote. The president will direct the EAC to subtract grant funds from any state that uses private funds to run public elections, so that unfair election interference can be minimized.

**5. Direct the US Postal Service to charge states a higher rate for ballot-related mail.** Vote-by-mail is recognized internationally as uniquely vulnerable to fraud and interference. The federal government cannot stop states from using it, but it can discourage states from doing so by raising the price for the postage of ballots. If Third World countries have voters show up in person, there is no reason that Americans should be unable to do so.

**6. Audit state voter rolls.** State voter rolls have been found to be rife with errors, ineligible voters, and other problems. The Trump administration will direct investigators from the Department of Justice and the Treasury to conduct thorough audits of each state's processes for registering voters, maintaining voter rolls, and verifying voter identity. States that reject audits will be ineligible for EAC funding grants; federal taxpayers should not subsidize election fraud.

**7. Audit election results.** There is no reason that election results should not be available for audit so that the public can be assured that ballots were cast properly and counted correctly. The Treasury will be directed to work with states on developing methods to make verification of voting results easy and transparent, and to ensure that recounts do not take inordinately long. Unless the public can trust the results of elections, we cannot restore faith in our democracy.

# Chapter 11

# Conclusion

The agenda I have described above is one that a newly inaugurated President Donald Trump can implement on Day One of his second administration. But it is only the beginning: there is much more that Trump can achieve if he is able to work with Congress to pass legislation that implements his agenda. If Republicans have majorities in both houses of Congress, and can convince enough Democrats to overcome the Senate filibuster, they can aim even higher:

**1. Fully fund the border wall and overhaul the country's immigration system.** Democrats shut down the government in 2019 rather than fund the border wall—and the result is clear. Congress can pass the necessary funding to secure the southern border completely. They can reform our nation's immigration laws—once and for all—to admit those who deserve to be here and remove those who do not. If border security is achieved, immigration reform is possible.

**2. Fund an expanded US Navy; develop the Space Force and AI warfare aggressively.** The US is not prepared for the threat that China poses to American security, allies, and interests. Congress should fund the expansion of the US naval fleet to catch up to China's rapid naval armament. It should also fund a Space Force that can dominate the "final frontier," and should accelerate military research into artificial intelligence (AI) for use in warfare.

**3. Fund new national monuments and the national bicycle trail.** As noted above, the administration can develop plans for a museum of communism, the Garden of Heroes, and a national bicycle trail—but only Congress can fund them. If Trump succeeded in pushing the Great American Outdoors Act through Congress in 2020—a rare bipartisan achievement on national parks, in a divisive year—he can bring the parties together again for similar lofty goals.

**4. Move toward balanced federal budgets.** Many of the steps described in earlier chapters show how President Trump can plan for balanced budgets by proposing cuts to government departments, threatening to veto budgets that do not return unspent funds to the fiscus, and so on. But he can only follow through on these plans if Congress does its part. There will be back-and-forth, and negotiations, but it can be done: it has been done before, in living memory.

**5. Restructure the nation's debt and reform entitlement programs.** As with budgets, the president can only fulfill his proposals on debt and entitlement reform if Congress agrees. The changes ought to be bipartisan, if possible, as successful reforms have been in the past. But if necessary, the president and Republicans should be prepared to pass these reforms on their own, because the nation's financial security, and eventually its physical security, are at stake.

**6. Fund paid maternity leave and other child-friendly policies.** America needs to invest in children if we are to have a future, both culturally and financially. While the initial outlay might be expensive, paid maternity leave will pay for itself over time, both in terms of increased revenues from working mothers, and eventual contributions by children who grow up to be productive citizens. Congress can also pass laws to block abuse of the system by those who do not work.

**7. End the immunity of Silicon Valley social media platforms.** It is time to repeal Section 230 of the Communications Decency Act, under which the social media companies have enjoyed broad immunity from lawsuits about their management of content on Internet platforms. In addition, Congress should pass laws to regulate the rapidly-growing field of AI, bringing it within ethical boundaries and protecting American workers from losing their livelihood to algorithms.

President Trump will, undoubtedly, face some of the same opponents he faced in his first term, when the so-called "Resistance" sprang up to challenge every new policy of his administration. The same forces are already mobilizing across the country—bankrolled by shadowy donors, sometimes living abroad, who funnel millions through a cascade of non-profit organizations that recruit, train, and deploy activists on the street, and fund lawsuits and media smear campaigns.

We can see their presence already on the streets of America. They have used the October 7 terror attack by Hamas against Israel—which electrified the pro-Palestinian movement—to sharpen their tactics and expand their reach. They intend to pick up where they left off in 2020, when left-wing groups planned to shut down the country in the event a close election pointed to Trump as the winner. Their goal is not political change but to make the country ungovernable.

The Biden administration has studiously avoided

investigating these activists and the donors who fund them—because they are often the same donors funding Biden's reelection effort and Democratic Party campaigns more generally. Ideally, the Department of Justice would already have launched Racketeer Influenced and Corrupt Organizations (RICO) investigations of these left-wing networks, as well as civil rights investigations into their antisemitism and bigotry.

The Trump administration will have to start those investigations from scratch. In the meantime, the new administration may have to invoke the Insurrection Act and deploy the military to stop the radical left from disrupting the government and undermining the peaceful transfer of power. Democrats will complain—but these are the same Democrats who put up barbed-wire fences around the Capitol and sent troops into the streets for the first several months under Joe Biden.

There should also be consequences for those who support the "Resistance" in the mainstream media with fawning coverage and, as in 2020, active participation. The Trump White House was too willing, in its first term, to work with media outlets that were working with the forces trying to bring him down. Hostile outlets, no matter how prominent, should be shunned, and the press corps should be moved out of its plush West Wing perch to separate premises, if necessary.

While the actions should be firm and forceful, the rhetoric of the new Trump administration should be conciliatory, where possible. Words can be cheap: when President Biden delivered his Inaugural Address, for example, he used the word "unity" eight times. He never meant it. But Trump can combine messages of reconciliation with outreach to Democrats willing to work with him on specific issues—perhaps Sen. John Fetterman (D-PA) or Rep. Richie Torres (D-NY).

Nothing is quite as convincing as success—and as the Trump administration's policies take root, and begin to deliver for the American people as they did before, public support for the new administration will grow. The radical forces in the street today, after all, are not only anti-Israel but explicitly anti-American, and even anti-Christian. They tear down the flag; they interrupt Christmas tree lightings; they target anything seen as a symbol of mainstream American culture.

The key is to isolate the "Resistance," expose its true beliefs, and uncover the financial and political networks that allow it to dominate American political discourse even though it only represents a tiny minority of people, largely in far-left cities. The confrontation that is coming is largely a test of wills, and it must be absolutely clear from the outset that while the new Trump administration has an open door to Democrats, it is committed to stopping the radical left.

☆ ☆ ☆

It is, of course, possible that Trump will lose the election. As I complete this book—now on Tuesday, January 11, just ten days after I began—Trump is slightly favored to win, according to the experts at DecisionDesk. He leads President Biden in several swing-state polls, and even has a slim national lead of 0.5 percent, according to the RealClearPolitics average of polls. If his enemies hoped to use his conviction in New York to damage his chances, they have failed.

A year ago, perhaps, it would have been unthinkable for Trump to be in such a strong position. The indictments, state and federal, were piling up, and had not yet fully been exposed as the shams that they are. The Capitol riot of January 6, 2021, still cast a long shadow over Trump and his supporters. Trump faced what looked like it might be a serious primary challenge from Florida Gov. Ron DeSantis, a former Trump endorsee who emerged as a Republican superstar.

But the prosecutions made Trump stronger. They identified him as the leader of the opposition, and, over time, exposed the corruption of a government that would stoop to Banana Republic tactics to destroy a political rival. President Biden's frailties became impossible to ignore, as did the crisis at the southern border—one entirely of Biden's own making. Biden's weakness on the world stage was reinforced by the October 7 Hamas terror attack. His polls continued to fall.

Still, it is unclear that Americans' desire for change will be reflected at the ballot box. Many voters are convinced that the changes pushed by Democrats in 2020—universal vote-by-mail, for example—put Republicans at a permanent disadvantage. The media remain hostile to Trump and his supporters, and often fail to report on many of the administration's worst failures. Democrats are set to renominate Biden, despite his flaws, because they think he can win.

I believe that Trump has a chance to win, but I also still believe that Biden is the favorite. So many forces are arrayed against Trump that only a massive turnout of Trump voters can put him over the top. He may have help from third-party candidates—perhaps Robert F. Kennedy, Jr. Kennedy appeals to Trump supporters but will likely take more votes away from Biden, among Democrats who don't want him reelected but who cannot bring themselves to vote for Trump.

If Biden wins, it will be a hollow victory. Half the country, at least, will see the election as having been illegitimate, "rigged" by phony prosecutions that were delayed until election season. Most of the charges would never have been filed against someone not named "Trump," and seemed to have been filed either to force Trump out of the race, or else to tag him with a "felon" label. Rejection of the 2024 results would be wider—and more justified—than the "denial" of 2020.

Furthermore, the country will be more difficult for Biden to govern—not because Republicans will riot in the streets, as leftists do, or take up arms against the government, but rather because many ordinary Americans will simply conclude that democracy does work, and that they cannot win. They will simply stop participating in self-government, and contribute less to society, finding solace in family, in private amusements, or in simple isolation, as they await an uncertain future.

Writers from Alexis de Tocqueville to Ayn Rand have warned of the potential for individual retreat from public affairs. Democracy depends on more than voting; it depends on self-government, and the willingness of citizens to engage in public affairs out of an enlightened sense of self-interest. If people sense that their efforts are wasted, they will quit, quietly. Our society will become less productive, less dynamic, less adaptable—and more vulnerable to conquest.

☆ ☆ ☆

When Trump won in 2016, against the odds and defying nearly every expert prediction, I marveled at the power of American democracy to renew itself. The political establishment expected that a Hillary Clinton victory would cement the foundations of the "progressive" oligarchy in Washington, DC. The millenarian candidacy and presidency of Barack Obama, which marked the end of politics for many of his supporters, would essentially never end.

Trump disrupted all of that. He prevented the Supreme Court from falling into liberal hands and becoming the vanguard of the left as it sought to impose a doctrine of socioeconomic rights on constitutional jurisprudence. Trump slowed—and, for a few short years, reversed—the decline of the United States as a world power, winning a trade war with China, holding Russia at bay, supporting freedom in Latin America, and even forging new peace deals in the Middle East.

The fact that citizens could still make choices in the privacy of the voting booth, regardless of the polls and the pundits, proved the enduring virtue of democracy. Without Trump, without the freedom of choice that his victory represented, many necessary but difficult policies never would have come about. Even determined opponents of Trump had to concede that the Abraham Accords, for example, were a stunning achievement—one that only Trump could have made.

That is why the political establishment did everything possible to limit choice in the 2020 election. They exploited a pandemic to shut down public gatherings, and to impose a new vote-by-mail system that matched the Democrats' preferred mechanism for turning out their own voters. Leaders in government and business endorsed violent protests that threatened to topple the country. They suppressed bad news about Biden and censored criticism on social media.

The same forces have been deployed in the 2024 election, and the next few months will see new and extraordinary tactics to keep Trump from returning to the White House. And yet the polls are telling us something very important—a story about the resilience of popular will, about the dogged refusal of millions of Americans to accept the political conformity that is being imposed upon them, about the determination of the American people to fight for their country.

They do not see all of their hopes and aspirations embodied in one man. This is not a cult of personality, though certainly Trump is one of the most charismatic figures in American political history. People understand Trump's flaws, and even many of his supporters quietly wonder whether he is too old—seventy-eight years old, just three years younger than Biden—or whether he has been so damaged by his trials that he will govern in a spirit of personal revenge, not public duty.

Trump was an enigma when he took office in 2017, but the world will know what it is getting if he takes office in 2025. The same tactics that made Trump's first term so successful may not work a second time. The America he inherits will be much weaker than he left it—deeper debt; higher interest rates; more crime; fewer children; a lack of soldiers; and a flood of illegal aliens.

And the country will be more bitterly divided than it has been since the end of the Civil War.

Yet if Trump enters office with a clear agenda, such as the one I have outlined above, he can set the tone for a presidency that will overcome the supposed weaknesses of a lame-duck term and begin to turn America around. The key is to have the right plans, carried out by the right people, in the quickest time possible. The first 100 days of the second Trump term could be the most important of any president—a turning point, saving the United States from the abyss.